Museums as Assemblage

Museums as Assemblage offers a new way of thinking about the dynamism of art museums.

Using the concept of assemblage, this book unpacks relations between visitors, artists, museum staff, and the museum's nonhuman components, providing an analytical framework that celebrates the complexity of museums today. It takes the Museum of Old and New Art (Mona) in Tasmania as its primary case study but situates it in global trends by drawing on a range of examples from art museums across Australia, New Zealand, Europe, and East Asia. It provides insight into how perceptions around engagement are enabled and constrained in the context of different museums and highlights the necessity of an analytical framework that accommodates the complexity and multiplicity of the contemporary museum landscape.

With an emphasis on visitor experience and curatorial strategy, the book is valuable for students and researchers in museum studies, art history, curatorial studies, and cultural studies.

Jasmin Pfefferkorn is a postdoctoral research fellow in The University of Melbourne's School of Culture and Communication. Her research centres on museum studies, aesthetics, digital and computational cultures, media and communications, and visual culture. She is the co-founder of the research group *CODED AESTHETICS* and teaches master's students in global media communications and arts and cultural management.

Museums in Focus
Series Editor: Kylie Message
Australian National University, Australia

Committed to the articulation of big, even risky ideas, in small format publications, 'Museums in Focus' challenges authors and readers to experiment with, innovate, and press museums and the intellectual frameworks through which we view these. It offers a platform for approaches that radically rethink the relationships between cultural and intellectual dissent and crisis and debates about museums, politics and the broader public sphere.

'Museums in Focus' is motivated by the intellectual hypothesis that museums are not innately 'useful', safe' or even 'public' places, and that recalibrating our thinking about them might benefit from adopting a more radical and oppositional form of logic and approach. Examining this problem requires a level of comfort with (or at least tolerance of) the idea of crisis, dissent, protest and radical thinking, and authors might benefit from considering how cultural and intellectual crisis, regeneration and anxiety have been dealt with in other disciplines and contexts.

The following list includes only the most-recent titles to publish within the series. A list of the full catalogue of titles is available at: https://www.routledge.com/Museums-in-Focus/book-series/MIF

Museums as Assemblage
Analysing Dynamic Museum Practice
Jasmin Pfefferkorn

Self-Determined First Nations Museums and Colonial Contestation
The Keeping Place
Robert Hudson and Shannon Woodcock

⌐MUSEUMS IN FOCUS⌐

Logo by James Verdon (2017)

Museums as Assemblage

Analysing Dynamic Museum Practice

Jasmin Pfefferkorn

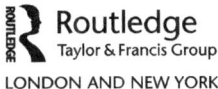

LONDON AND NEW YORK

First published 2024
by Routledge
4 Park Square, Milton Park, Abingdon, Oxon OX14 4RN

and by Routledge
605 Third Avenue, New York, NY 10158

Routledge is an imprint of the Taylor & Francis Group, an informa business

© 2024 Jasmin Pfefferkorn

British Library Cataloguing-in-Publication Data
A catalogue record for this book is available from the British Library

ISBN: 978-1-032-49204-9 (hbk)
ISBN: 978-1-032-49420-3 (pbk)
ISBN: 978-1-003-39371-9 (ebk)

DOI: 10.4324/9781003393719

Typeset in Times New Roman
by Apex CoVantage, LLC

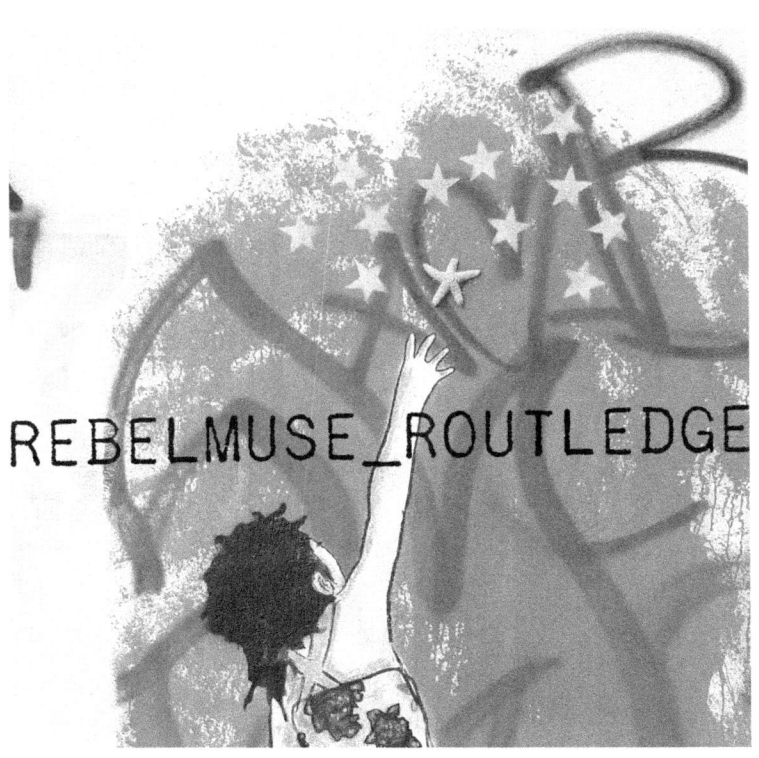

REBELMUSE_ROUTLEDGE

Contents

Figures

Acknowledgements

Many people have supported me on my journey as an early-career researcher. A big thank you to Nikos Papastergiadis and Scott McQuire, who have been my champions at The University of Melbourne. Thank you to my colleague and collaborator Emilie K. Sunde – sharing an office with you is immensely joyful.

I'd like to acknowledge the research done by the ARC team – Adrian, Justin, Nikos, Scott, Miriam, and Kate – with whom this project first originated back in 2013. I'd also like to thank both Kylie Message and Heeranshi Sharma for their brilliant editing work at Routledge. Thanks to Charles Esche and Tony Holzner for allowing me to ask them a million and one questions.

Thank you to my wonderful family – Els Daglinckx, Dieter Pfefferkorn, Jarran Pfefferkorn, Sara Broadhurst, and John Holyoake. And, of course, to my biggest cheerleaders – Ruby Awburn and Mirai Hinchy-Kirsanovs.

My deepest gratitude goes to Josh Broadhurst. Thank you for all you do.

Introduction

Take a look at art museum operations, their curatorial strategies, a visitor's experience. Can you make a sweeping statement that these emerge in the same way across all art museums today? Go deeper and focus on just one museum. Do the objects, artworks, people, policies, media, and site come together and interact in the same way every time you look? Traditionally, museums have been viewed as relatively fixed, stable, and slow-changing institutions. And yet, the global contemporary context is shaped more by motion than it is by stasis. To make sense of museums today necessitates a change in perspective – one that takes dynamism as a focal point.

Around the world, new relationships between museums are formed, some highly corporatised, others founded in a sense of the commons (Papastergiadis 2020). Art museum visitors and professionals – as well as artworks, artists, and collections – are networked, manifesting different ideas, social relations, and local–global connections. The institutional critique of museum, questioning their role and function in society, has been building over the last half century. The future of the museum is something that has been speculated, counselled, and despaired. There have been demands by academics, artists, museum professionals, government bodies, and publics to make the museum more inclusive, more collaborative, and more interesting. Simultaneously, the tensions and limitations faced by museums – funding models and a lack of resources, balancing multiple and at times conflicting roles and publics – have been emphasised in museum studies literature.

While many features of traditional museums have been perceived as destabilised – cultural authority, strict governance, and top-down knowledge dissemination, as well as positioning the visitor as an art-worshipful spectator – these practices and ideologies continue to be discernible in museums today. Recently founded museums use curatorial strategies that invoke Renaissance Wunderkammer theatricality and polysemy (Bann 2008). Museums that privilege a sensory experience over a conventionally educative experience are not necessarily more interactive – while some do have tangible displays, others remain ocular-centric (Candlin 2010). Private museums and house museums are on the rise and often collaborate with government bodies

DOI: 10.4324/9781003393719-1

(Walker 2019). Many museums aim for democracy and inclusion but continue to draw on Enlightenment rationales or project colonialist ideology (Black 2021). Visitors are often encouraged to embody several modes of spectatorship and participation within a single exhibition (McSweeney and Kavanagh 2016). The site of the museum extends beyond its physical walls, becoming a navigation of digital space as well as place (Kidd 2014).

Museum studies as a discipline has tended towards positioning museums as fixed, bound by a particular historical moment and location. What has resulted are a series of museum 'categories' that underemphasise how museum practice is simultaneously changing and continuous. It is in a context of heightened flux and increased social demands that the Museum of Old and New Art (Mona) in Hobart, Tasmania, emerged. A private museum founded in 2011 by David Walsh, Mona doesn't fit neatly inside any pre-existing museum category. As such, it has been described as a 'unique museum experience' (Olszanka 2011), with 'simply nothing like it on Earth' (Salmon 2016) and as an 'anti-museum' (Franklin 2014, 2020). And yet, when positioned in a global context, Mona isn't an isolated phenomenon. Nor is it unique in problematising the way we define and attempt to analyse the museum. When we look at museums in the contemporary context, we see that the fixed perspective doesn't adequately represent the conditions of the museum. The difficulty in fixing Mona within a singular museum model, typology, category, or definition is emblematic of a wider narrative; museums are more dynamic than ever before. We need only look at the highly contested process of settling on a new definition of museums instigated by the International Council of Museums (ICOM) in 2019. With over 250 proposals, this process was indicative of the multiple and diverse ways in which museums and their role in society are perceived. It is in this shifting landscape that I propose a new analytical approach to the study of museums (Chapter 2). My approach draws on the prominent work of Deleuze and Guattari (1987) on assemblage theory. Reading their work led me to wonder what an assemblage theory approach to analysing museums would illuminate. Would taking a methodology renowned for its capacity to trace things in motion allow me to mirror the dynamism I was seeing in museums? What new connections would this make both across and within museums? This book offers a foundational mapping of museums as assemblage. It is not intended to be wholly comprehensive, nor should it be. The assemblage only thrives when we avoid totalisation.

The following chapter provides an introduction to Mona and a brief survey of Mona's diverse practices. It demonstrates the way in which these practices do not fit into a neat framework of museum practice. It highlights how, on a temporal and spatial scale, Mona cannot be confined within a singular museum model or category. Through participant observation, interviews, and Mona's social media engagement, I explored how Mona's success has led to intersections with other assemblages (government, publics, and other museums).

Mona continues to be celebrated as radical and anti-museum. I provide an alternative narrative that illustrates the way in which Mona oscillates between its unconventional origin and its cumulative institutionalisation.

To position dynamism in a wider framework, I then set up four museum 'common notions'. Deleuze writes that a 'common notion' is defined as 'an idea of similarity of composition in existing modes' (1990: 275). These develop into systems of relations that are reified through habitual practice. In later works, he notes that 'common notions are not abstract, they are collective, they always refer to a multiplicity, but they're no less individual for that' (Deleuze 2007). According to John Phillips (2006: 109), a common notion is a representation for bodies that have something in common entering into a relationship or composition that can be seen as an independent unity. A common notion is that which allows us to recognise an assemblage as a stable or whole object or body. We perceive these in the museum when the human and non-human components come together and interact in ways that affirm each other. A common notion is simultaneously collective and individual (transindividual), common to the whole and common to the part. The assemblages I outline are distinctive because the 'museum bodies' within each form a common notion. An assemblage can then be differentiated from the common notion, as it is the process of becoming, rather than the perception of the stable whole.

In this book, I locate four common notions – the normative (Chapter 3), the responsive (Chapter 4), the affective (Chapter 5), and the emergent (Chapter 6). A normative museum common notion will have informational wall placards written by curators, prescribed linear movement, permanent collections, policies for visitor behaviour enforced by invigilators, and so on. These come together to affirm the idea of a museum as an authoritative institution, where visitors are positioned as art-worshipful spectators. The normative museum is characterised by a long spatio-temporal trajectory and is often expressed as a 'traditional' museum. These are our white cube exhibition formats, our art historical narratives, and our conception of museums as repositories of history, authoritative information and object-artwork conservation. As a result, the normative museum also plays a public service role, becoming an intermediary for the State, a representational body of the nation, an educational institution. A responsive common notion is more community oriented – it holds space for the changing needs of its publics and is willing to relinquish some control over its operations through collaborations. The responsive museum is that which takes community responsibility at the heart of its practice, focusing on visitors as constituents. The responsive museum is seen to have shifted its practices as a result of the 'culture wars', to refocus on post-colonialist narratives. However, the responsive museum (like the normative) positions the visitor within the category of 'audience' and encourages a top-down pedagogy (though with a stronger sense of the multiplicity of narratives and a diversity of visitor needs).

An affective common notion privileges the sensory over other forms of knowing. Perhaps there are no wall placards and more emphasis is placed on evocative stage-setting. Affective museums shift away from the pedagogic, moralising, and 'top-down' approach of exhibits to a focus on spectacle, immersive experience, and atmospherics. At its most reductive interpretation, the affective museum may be interpreted as playing a vital role in the experience/entertainment economy (think the installation-based art museums that revolve around 'Instagram-able' exhibitions).

An emergent common notion is inherently unstable – curatorial strategies are highly experimental, and it operates at a different temporality, with alterations occurring in real-time. In other words, in perceiving the emergent common notion, the visitor comes to expect the unexpected. The emergent[1] museum is that which, rather than the 'control and contain' strategy utilised by many museums (seen to preserve and enhance authority and legitimacy, and assist in territorialising the assemblage), encourages open systems of interaction. This may be located in the various affordances of digital media to create a feedback loop between visitors and professionals, more autonomy in visitor movement, and less cohesion regarding the overarching role, mission, and speculated trajectory of the museum. While all museums are in varying states of becoming, the emergent museum moves at a more rapid pace, as it is self-reflexive in regard to its own becoming. Unlike other museum assemblages, the sense of the emergent museum is that its boundaries are always – and necessarily – blurred. It allows for its components to move fluidly within and out of the assemblage. The emergent museum is more dynamic and flexible as a result.

The way that the components of the museum assemblage interact is what creates the perception of a museum as a particular common notion. And yet, there is such variety in the way components combine and interactions occur. It is important to stress that assemblages are not essentialist categories. Essentialism begins with a finished product, looks at the enduring properties that characterise the product, and makes these properties into 'essences' that define the product. While we can discern common characteristics that position a museum within a common notion, museum practice is subject to change, and, as such, museums have the potential to move from embodying one common notion to another, particularly when component interactions take a particular direction over a sustained period, and at every level of the museum. For instance, what was once perceived as a normative museum may be reterritorialised as affective, or vice versa. I begin with the museums' components, tracing how they relate to one another to form the assemblage, rather than beginning with the museum as a stable whole. This constant process of 'becoming' speaks to the capacity for the museum assemblage to reconfigure itself, through a multitude of potential trajectories.

The provocation for this line of thinking came from my time spent at Mona. The goal here is not to develop a critical appraisal of the perceived 'success' of Mona. Rather, it is to problematise that idea of a 'unique cultural phenomenon', situating Mona within a wider scope of both contemporary and historical practice within art museums. While claims to Mona's distinctiveness are not without merit, it is part of a complex network of museum interactions. Tracing these interactions and their relational qualities allows us to think about how and why museums produce, and are produced by, varying intensities of change and continuity. What Mona offers as a case study is an insight into contradictions. Mona does not fit neatly into a singular typology or a linear historical narrative. It combines progressive marketing strategies and entrepreneurial motives with public services and community programmes. It rebels against an art-worshipful spectatorship by incorporating self-reflexive, playful and even parodic, language in communicating about the artworks and the role of museums. Architecturally, however, it holds features symbolic of the museum as 'temple', and visitors are encouraged to enact different forms of spectatorship and engagement through different exhibitions. Mona defies boundaries of museological analysis in quite an overt way, a notion given further weight by the hype around Mona as a 'cultural phenomenon'.

Analysis of Mona seems to indicate component interactions that play to normative, responsive, affective, and emergent practices. Isolated from the interactions with powerful assemblage systems – governmental, social, and economic – Mona retains its emergent practices. The reality, however, is that these other assemblage systems are re-territorialising some of the processes within Mona towards normative and responsive practices, with Mona very much a participant in this process. For the time being, Mona retains the perception of an emergent museum assemblage – dynamic, flexible, reactive, and continuing to afford a greater capacity for its various components to affect one another. As I worked towards positioning Mona within the wider context of contemporary museum practice, I found that most museums blur the boundaries and exceed the linear narrative often expressed in the field of museum studies.

In an era characterised by contemporaneity and global flows, what appear to be 'singularities' can instead be viewed as 'universal singularities', the result of a complex interplay of components that slot in and out of museum assemblages. The issue we face with existing museum typologies is that they are not fluid enough to maintain their relevancy in the face of dynamic relations. Alongside more recent institutional critique by academics, artists, and museum professionals, I consider museum practice through a lens of complexity and relationality. When we take historical significance, the influence of individuals, wider social, political, cultural, and economic systems, and the ways in which interactions between museum components configure museum practice, we see that museums comprise multidirectional flows of relations.

The way I have conceived of multiplicity allows for a more pluralistic, rather than fragmented, understanding of culture. In this, I have engaged with the museum assemblage as a set of circumstances. Assemblage systems theory is based on the principle that the virtual is always actualised through the act of conceiving it. In this book, I give the function of theory a different meaning by applying an assemblage systems methodology to museology. I have endeavoured to unlock theory from its authoritative and structural foundation, offering it dynamic lines of flight. By repositioning theory as a force that traces rather than captures complex interactions, I leave space for ambiguity, becoming, and potentiality in museum practice.

The assemblage systems approach intensifies an already complex area of analysis. It is worth pursuing as a methodology that simultaneously formulates a conceptual framework, while also accommodating modes of becoming and potentiality. What I have aimed to achieve is not only a convincing argument for why this conceptual framework is valuable but also an illustration of how this framework can be implemented in the critical analysis of museum practice. I am not unaware of the irony of occupying a position of double identity, whereby I actualise a self-reflexivity to renegotiate thinking in relation to museums while developing 'common notions' to accommodate universal singularities. Regardless, I believe that the underpinning of assemblage and flux throughout this body of work speaks louder than the boundaries I have created to make sense of multiplicity.

By honouring the concept of potentiality, it is my intention that readers of this work will feel their capacities for affect and imaginative percept enhanced. For museum professionals and visitors alike, this reveals how components exercise their capacity in both material and expressive roles. The complexity of these relations situates both human and non-human components of museums in a position where they both affect and are affected. As such, it can be seen as an aide for locating spaces for affect, which may lead to creative, imaginative, and productive enunciations of capacity. For those who study and write on museums, the complexity of potentiality may be daunting, but it is equally liberating, eliciting unexpected connections. Taking a focus on the relational interactions of components welcomes the constant states of negotiation we find in these spaces. In this, it is my hope that scholars taking up the work of analysing museum practices will find value in the critical language I have developed.

Note

1   I use the term 'emergent' to describe this assemblage common notion, not to be synonymous with 'contemporary', but rather to describe a state of motion and flux implicit within emergent museum practices.

References

Bann, Steven (2008). The Return to Curiosity: Shifting Paradigms in Contemporary Museum Display'. A. McClellen (ed.) *Art and its Publics: Museum Studies at the Millennium.* Oxford: Blackwell Publishing Ltd. Pp. 117–130.

Black, Graham (ed.) (2021). *Museums and the Challenge of Change: Old Institutions in a New World*. London/New York: Routledge.

Candlin, Fiona (2010). *Art, Museums and Touch*. Manchester: Manchester University Press.

Deleuze, Giles (1990). *Expressionism in Philosophy: Spinoza*. New York: Zone Books.

Deleuze, Giles (2007). 'On Spinoza'. https://deleuzelectures.blogspot.com/2007/02/onspinoza.html, last accessed 7 February 2017.

Deleuze, Gilles and Felix Guattari (1987 [1980]). *A Thousand Plateaus*. B. Massumi (trans.). London: Continuum.

Franklin, Adrian (2014). *The Making of MONA*. UK: Penguin.

Franklin, Adrian (2020). *Anti-Museum*. Oxon/New York: Routledge.

Kidd, Jenny (2014). *Museums in the New Mediascape: Transmedia, Participation, Ethics*. Surrey/Burlington: Ashgate Publishing, Ltd.

McSweeney, Kayte and Jen Kavanagh (eds.) (2016). *Museum Participation: New Directions for Audience Collaboration*. Edinburgh, UK: MuseumsEtc.

Olszanka, Paulina (2011). 'Hobart's New Gallery/Freak Show: Quintessentially Aussie, if a Little Absurd'. *Crikey*, 25 January 2011. https://www.crikey.com.au/2011/01/25/hobartsnew-galleryfreakshowquintessentially-aussie-if-a-little-absurd/, last accessed 26 December 2016.

Papastergiadis, Nikos (2020). *Museum of the Commons: L'Internationale and the Crisis of Europe*. London: Routledge.

Phillips, John (2006). 'Agencement/assemblage'. *Theory Culture and Society* 23(2/3). Pp. 108–109.

Salmon, Gregor (2016). 'Capital Gains: How MONA Got Hobart Humming'. *ABC News*, 4 October 2016. https://www.abc.net.au/news/2016-01-13/mona-got-hobart-humming/, last accessed 12 October 2016.

Walker, Georgina S. (2019). *The Private Collector's Museum: Public Good versus Private Gain*. London: Routledge.

1 Contemporary Museum Practice

The Museum of Old and New Art

The Museum of Old and New Art (Mona) is perceived as emerging from geographic and ideological peripheries. Located in the largely working-class suburb of Glenorchy, on the fringe of Hobart in Tasmania, the museum opened in 2011 with a distinct thematic focus on 'sex and death'. Mona has developed a cultural capital that does not rely on traditional formalities pre-existing in art museums. The relatively transgressive artworks on display, the dark subterranean architecture (see Figure 1.1), and its anti-authoritarian stance, all serve to heighten the art museum's allure. As a private museum, Mona does not have the same funding model as public museums, nor the same reliance on external governing bodies. Mona is not driven by conventional policy. The strategies in play through its development can be regarded as important markers of a 'reinvented' art museum. And yet, Mona is not exempt from increasingly institutionalised practices. These factors, combined with its unprecedented popularity, make Mona fertile ground for an analysis of contemporary museum practice. This chapter offers a brief overview of Mona's priorities, resources, publics, and processes[1] in order to illustrate its dynamic nature.

Mona's Priorities

Mona does not have a mission statement. David Walsh, Mona's owner-collector, has offered numerous and – at times contradictory – statements regarding his motivation in building a museum. In the first edition of *Monanisms* (2010),[2] Walsh writes that Mona is 'the bizarre outcome of a random process'. In the second edition, perhaps not entirely jokingly, Walsh states, 'Better build a museum. Make myself famous. That'll get the chicks' (Walsh 2013: xii). In his autobiography he writes, 'It's fair to argue that I built Mona to absolve myself from feeling guilty about making money without making a mark' (Walsh 2014: 97). Walsh himself has claimed that he reverse-engineered a sense of mission and priorities. However, as stated on the Mona website, to look towards Walsh for answers 'is to fall foul of the "narrative fallacy": the tendency to seek pattern when there is none, and to assume earlier events caused later ones in a way that confirms what we already believed about the

DOI: 10.4324/9781003393719-2

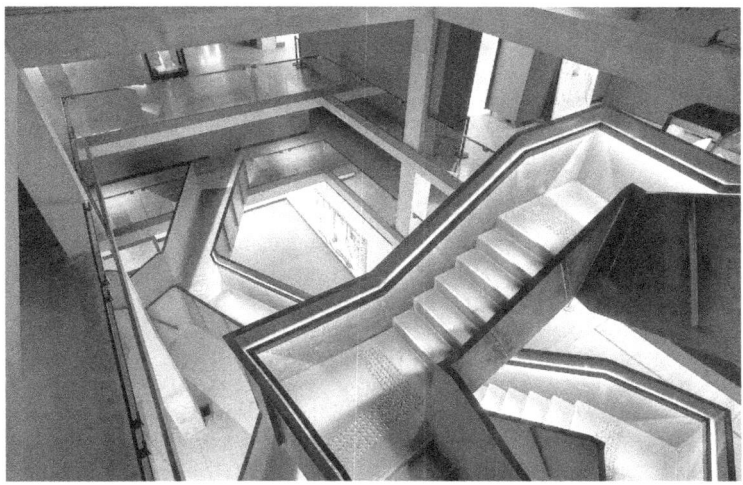

Figure 1.1 Photograph of Mona's 'labyrinth-like' interior.

Image courtesy of Museum of Old and New Art, Hobart, Tasmania, Australia.

world' (Mona: Introduction n.d.). Nonetheless, Walsh's role is integral to how the museum has been realised. There is a parallel between Walsh, his statements, and the practices of Mona: they are difficult to pin down. Another avenue of exploration in how Mona's priorities are negotiated is through its hybrid roles as commercial enterprise and public service.

What exists in place of a museum mission statement are records of Mona's brand vision.[3] In an email exchange with Leigh Carmichael,[4] Walsh wrote about the diversity of offerings at Mona (from art and architecture to food and wine), with every offering 'informed by a deep attachment to the principles of humanism'. He also wrote of his goal to provide both an emotional and intellectual engagement that would make a 'permanent impression on the mindscape' (Franklin 2014: 78). Embedded in this statement is that Mona combines commercial and philanthropic drives, offering products and services while retaining 'principles of humanism'. At a time where art museums attempt to balance their commercial emphasis with older cultural ideals, the private museum takes on a particularly interesting role. Walsh has been exceedingly upfront about the freedom he holds, relative to a public gallery. This perception that private museums do not have the same limitations as public museums lends credibility to the idea that private museums are better equipped to take on emergent practices. This is extended when we consider that Walsh is able to operate within a rapid-response rate of acquisitions, while publicly funded museums often have strict policies and bureaucratic procedures for procuring artworks. Mona's priorities still shift with time, alongside more sustained interactions with public and governmental assemblages.

When Mona first opened, the attitude of Walsh, publicly echoed by many of his staff, promoted a distinct nonchalance towards the desires of visitors and state bodies. Quite quickly, however, the success and popularity of Mona meant that 'it is no longer true or appropriate to claim that we don't care what other people think of us; what we do with what they think is the important and difficult part' (Pearce 2013a: xvii). The museum's popularity and role in the urban regeneration of arts-led tourism in Tasmania have led Mona to collaborate with Hobart City Council, Glenorchy Council, and Tourism Tasmania. As Mona begins to intersect and collaborate further with governmental assemblages, it will necessarily negotiate the relational interactions faced by public museums around public accountability, which are most noticeably reinforced in normative (see Chapter 3) and responsive (see Chapter 4) common notions.

Mona's initial proclamation of anti-authoritarianism has not altogether dissipated, particularly through its claims towards radicalism and the dismissal of convention. Mona now seeks to balance this anti-authoritarian position with the aforementioned collaboration with the authorities. An interesting duality emerges as a result, at times leading to inconsistencies and contradictions in how its values are communicated through practice. To this end, I want to highlight three of its purported brand values: egalitarianism, pedagogy, and pleasure (Franklin 2014: 167). Let us begin with the claim towards 'egalitarianism'. These claims are attached to Mona's location within a working-class suburb, free entry for locals, and its playful – at times derisive – commentary on the art world. Further, it offers a concurrent, arguably more accessible, narrative alongside its art historical explanations. This aims to provide information without estranging those who do not have a prior knowledge of art history and its movements. Still, many locals continue to feel alienated at Mona. Visitor demographics have remained largely aligned with art institutions worldwide, which show higher statistical representations of older, tertiary-educated visitors with a higher level of cultural capital.[5] In Kate Booth's study of the perceptions of Mona by Berriedale residents in the Glenorchy municipality, she found that accessibility at Mona largely adheres to 'familiar socioeconomic lines' (Booth et al. 2017: 10). Today, the gap of financial accessibility continues to widen. With Mona's continuing expansion, visitors are faced with spending additional money for further experiences within the museum space. For many, this delimits their capacity to experience all that Mona has to offer. Mona currently operates at a significant deficit (with Walsh making up the difference); the hope is that Mona will self-sustain. As a result, more commercial activities and products become incorporated into the Mona assemblage. As a component that both shapes and is shaped by the assemblage, the visitor assumes a hybrid role, as both guest and consumer. We see a tension here between Mona as enterprise and Mona's vision of egalitarianism.

Another hybridity playing into the visitor experience is evident in Mona's values of 'pedagogy and pleasure'. While 'pedagogy and pleasure' have at times been considered as either binary opposites or parallel initiatives within museum practice, Mona suggests that both are critical to the vision of the museum. As such, Mona's priorities are symbolic of a 'between space' where normative pedagogy and affective pleasure are practiced simultaneously. Emotional and intellectual engagement are prioritised with equal weight in creating a wholistic and resonant experience. As we move through this chapter, it becomes apparent that this approach forges ambiguous, hybrid, and fluid modalities for the museum visitor component. Rather than seeing pedagogy and pleasure as dualities in conflict, in the assemblage whole we recognise they complement one another.

Mona's Resources

To understand why the resources at Mona emerged in a way that was lauded as ground-breaking, we must briefly reflect on Walsh's first museum – The Moorilla Museum of Antiquities (MMoA), which was open to the public from 1999 to 2006. MMoA is important because it acted as a catalyst for the distinctive practices that would later come to define Mona. Although MMoA staff did not come from a museums or art background, when MMoA opened it, in Walsh's words, 'looked like every other museum' (Walsh 2014). Retrospectively, Walsh realised he had assumed the normative museum standard of presenting work in a 'neutral matrix', leading to white walls, with works labelled to 'communicate the profundity of their collections' (Walsh 2014: 183). The use of wall placards established several further 'normative' contingencies in the way museum resources were deployed. The wall placards were there to be read, which meant light was needed for reading them, which in turn meant the lighting requirements of MMoA were the same as the majority of museums worldwide, which in turn impacted the architecture, and so on. Resolving this issue would lead to a resource that would come to indisputably shape the rest of Mona's practices, as well as people's perception and experience of this museum. It is here that we turn to the 'O' device.

The 'O' Device

The 'O' (designed by creative technology company *Art Processors*, in collaboration with Mona) is an application based on a touch user interface (TUI), usually a smartphone. It is not limited by space constraints in the same way as a wall placard. It offers a variety of perspectives, prompts, and points of engagement in relation to each work, affording a multiplicity of narratives to emerge. The 'O' uses tracking technology to position and orientate the visitor in the gallery space, provide information and ideas on the art and objects, and provide a level of participation and interaction for the individual that feeds back into a wider pattern of exchange and experience.[6] Originally, the 'O' was pre-loaded onto an Apple iPhone offered to visitors upon entering the exhibition spaces. Now, visitors must load it themselves onto their smartphone. Unlike older museums, which retroactively designed websites, joined social networking sites, and added digital technology as a supplementary layer to pre-existing components, digital media components were considered a core resource for Mona from the outset.[7] Mona, as a digital native rather than adapting to digitisation, is indicative of how closely intertwined digital practices are with a physical site.

As the visitor moves through the exhibition space, the 'O's' geolocative function allows the visitor to see thumbnail images of artworks nearby. By touching on the image of an artwork, the visitor is given up to five options for further information. The first (and also the default screen – see Figure 1.2) is a 'Summary' page, which serves the same purpose as the normative wall placard. The second is the section titled 'Ideas', which generates one of several different prompts or questions for thinking about the artwork. The third is a traditional, art historical narrative titled 'Artwank', while the fourth is usually written from the perspective of Walsh and is titled 'Gonzo'. The final option is 'Listen', which ranges from an interview with the artist to a piece of music accompanying the work. For some of the temporary guest-curated exhibitions, the option of an Audio-tour appears on-screen, allowing the visitor to listen to the curator's thought-process.

This is not where engagement with the 'O' finishes. From its inception, the device has also offered the visitor the option of 'voting' on an artwork by pressing either 'Love' or 'Hate'. In the first iteration of the 'O', upon 'voting', the visitor received a statistic in turn, positioning their vote in relation to the perspectives of others. A 'Love' vote may have generated a comment like '1,120 humans had similarly warm and fuzzy feelings'. This process of voting on an artwork was later extended. Rather than provide statistics, it now allows visitors to provide their own comments, with a feature titled 'Thoughts?'. In turn, commenting will generate an anonymous, randomised comment from a previous visitor. Pressing 'Hate' on an artwork issues a provocation – 'Come on, tell us what you really think. . .'. By pressing 'Love', you may receive the prompt 'This could be more interesting if you left your thoughts'. Using the device is by no means compulsory, however the vast majority of visitors opt to experience Mona with the 'O'. Those who take the 'O' device can become encompassed in their own bubble. From my own experience and observation, visitors often begin reading about a particular artwork and move away from the work itself, while still locked into the 'O' screen. As such, visitors wandering through the space experience a strange mixture of isolation and sociality, eyes shifting between the artworks and the handheld screen. While the 'O' is seen by many visitors as 'distracting' (Pearce 2013b: 58), it remains a crucial component to building a wholistic experience. *Art Processors* Co-Founder,

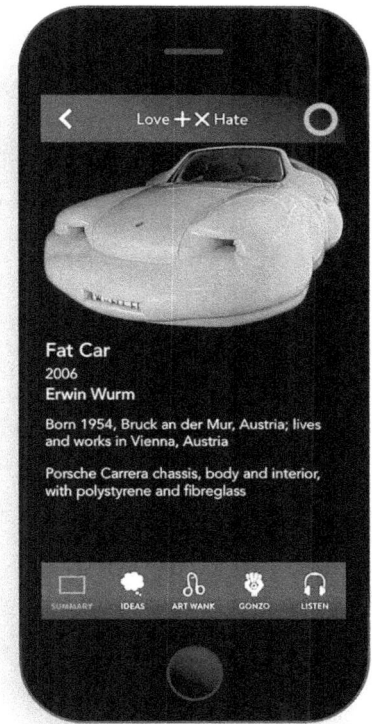

Figure 1.2 Image of the 'O' Device, showing a 'Summary' page that is the default display when a user clicks on an artwork thumbnail.

Image courtesy of Museum of Old and New Art, Hobart, Tasmania, Australia.

Tony Holzner (2022), speaks about noticing a trend over the last few years of moving away from screen-based approaches, with museums increasingly seeing themselves as a refuge away from the saturation of screens. The shift towards more requests for 'eyes up experiences' that are 'focused on audio' is seeing *Art Processors* moving into more 'atmospheric, almost cinematic audio experiences'. Audio was a part of the 'O' from its first iteration. Holzner (2022) states:

> Beyond just replacing wall text and lights, David Walsh wanted a medium that could provide lengthy written material and provide a lot of flexibility

to have multiple viewpoints. And by and large, that was written. And then there was another very important element, which was the interviews with artists in audio form, and that remains very successful. Those two different types of content have proven to really, really resonate with audiences.

The inherent flexibility of the 'O' means that it can be reactive to changing needs and socio-cultural developments. While the 'O' hasn't yet needed any major transformations, given how effective it has been in achieving desired outcomes, Holzner does say that this will change in the years to come, and that the next iteration of the 'O' will be more of a significant change.

Jenny Kidd's (2014) work on TUIs within museums highlights the value of positioning the museum visitor in relation to a wider community, which can create long-lasting and more nuanced memories of the exhibit as a result. As visitors move through the exhibition space, their own thoughts mingling with the 'Thoughts' of visitors who came before them, the 'O' affords them a sense of virtual sociality. One of the affordances of the 'O' is that it positions the visitors' individual experience in relation to the visitors who have come beforehand (through the options of 'voting' and 'Thoughts'). The individual visitor is positioned in relation to an invisible body of visitors who had at some level also engaged with an artwork enough to 'vote' on it. As a result of this virtual sociality, one is given an entry point to not only reflect on one's own experience but also to speculate on the experience of others. In this way visitors can communicate with other visitors to Mona across space and time. By providing a 'Thoughts' option beyond the voting of 'Love/Hate', Mona enhanced the visitor's capacity to heighten their expressive role through written comments. However, there is a sense that the shift from receiving statistics to being able to comment has impacted on some of the key benefits that the former produced in terms of virtual sociality. According to Holzner (2022):

> There's a move to go back to the original approach in terms of providing statistics, with the objective of allowing an individual visitor to see their view in relation to everyone else's. That was the goal there, it was 'here's what you thought, and you share the same perspective as 90% of the audience'. Or, more interestingly, you are an outlier to our typical visitor. Those ideas are important and that achieves a better effect.

Regardless, using the 'O' as a communicative tool generates possibilities for the circulation of ideas and knowledge beyond the content and strategies generated by museum staff. Walsh specified early on why he felt the affordances of the 'O' are important in relation to the visitor, linking user-provided content with the democratisation of the museum (Walsh 2014: 183).

If we consider that museum professionals have been traditionally understood as being the authoritative voice in knowledge production through museums, engagement with 'Thoughts' is indicative of the way in which visitors are renegotiating this position. Visitor feedback through the 'O' device can be understood as suggestive of the visitor's sense of their capacity to affect. The awareness of their own role moves away from that of 'transient, silent figures' (Hicks 2005: 66) or, in other words, a purely material component of the museum assemblage, to an expressive component. The consequences of this should not be underestimated. In studies of the visitor experience of museums, agency and ownership have been proven invaluable to the sustained role of museums in community-building (Hooper-Greenhill 2000; Kidd 2014). Feedback and interactive engagement within the museum space have been shown to produce experiences with longevity (Kidd 2014). That is, the communication that occurs in the museum is remembered beyond visitation.

The 'O' invokes both the literal and figurative definition of 'interface'. The interface can be understood as a device that enables a user to interact with a computer system, or more broadly as the meeting point between two systems of interaction. Consequently, the 'O' is explored here as a resource, and later as a process, though ultimately these are inextricable from one another. While the 'O's' hardware is a material resource, its content is expressive of Mona's priorities. When we look towards the 'O', we see that it holds the capacity for a non sequitur reading, the surface level of interaction is made up of distinctly traditional prompts. As a geo-locative app, it works in a sensemaking capacity, following moment-to-moment activity and connecting spaces. Its content communicates the collection and exhibition objects to the public, in ways that are expressive of Mona's priorities. The 'O' is also a data collection point for the visitors' time in the museum, accumulating individual data on movement through the exhibition spaces, time spent at different works, and in some cases, visitor response. If desired, visitors are able to save their visit and view it later to retrieve their pathway through the museum and information about artworks.

Understandably, the 'O' is a key area of interest in the scholarly work surrounding Mona (Franklin 2014, 2019; Carvalho 2017; Wilson-Barnao 2022). The focus tends to be on how curatorial strategies at Mona have been largely freed up due to the 'O' device. Lighting has been executed without needing to illuminate the traditional signage, allowing for black walls and unusual illumination schemes. The visitor, using the 'O' to guide them, is given an enhanced capacity to follow their own desire lines. Caroline Wilson-Barnao (2022) positions the 'O' as an 'open-ended cultural encounter', creating a feedback loop between museum and visitor. It is for good reason that the 'O' becomes a focal point for what we can understand as 'visitor feedback' in Mona. It holds a central role as a point of mediation for various types of interaction, as well as the data this generates. As a digital tool, the 'O' can be quickly updated, due to the aforementioned interactions that it facilitates across several of the museum's components. This in turn affects the relational interactions of these components. The value of the 'O' device in relation to the museum assemblage is that it affords Mona a rapid-response rate, a capacity to enact non-sequitur readings and aggregate user-generated content.

One of the features of the 'O' is its mapping capability, where visitor movements are traced through GIS tracking. Here, visitor feedback rests in the physicality of their movement patterns. While visitor movement varies from individual to individual, on a larger scale, patterns emerge. However, it is important not to overstate the museum's reactivity within this feedback loop. While early on it was Walsh's intention to remove the most 'loved' artworks from display, this became something that was phased out of the curatorial strategy, predominantly because the polarisation of response to artworks meant that the most loved were often also the most hated (Mona: Introduction n.d.). Reinforcing this, is Holzner's affirmation that very little is done with the 'O' data in terms of curation, given that in many ways 'data is after the fact' and, at Mona, 'the design of exhibitions always comes first and then content is layered, and then you get feedback about that' (Holzner: Interview 2022). It is instead the expressive role of virtual sociality *between visitors* in the space that has a greater application as a 'real-time' feedback loop.

Many museums are utilising digital technologies within their exhibition spaces in order to augment the visitor experience on site as well as provide data for museum professionals to utilise in their operational strategies. Mona takes on emergent characteristics through this process by utilising the 'O' for not only tracking, augmenting experience, and facilitating understanding of engagement and consumption but also to accommodate multiple modalities, subjectivities, and sociality. Falk et al. (2006) have long posited that the museum visitor takes on multiple modalities through their visitation, regardless of the component of digital technology within the museum. As such, while the 'O' heightens the affordances for facilitating visitor modalities and subjectivities, this function alone is not enough to be indicative of an emergent common notion. Instead, when considering Mona as emergent, it is the capacities of the 'O' for virtual sociality within the physical site of Mona that is key. This user-generated content evidences visitor feedback loops between a virtual body of visitors, rather than visitors and museum professionals. Within this aspect of the visitor–interface interaction we see dynamic, open feedback that extends beyond the modus operandi of 'control and containment' operations in many other museums.

When observing visitors approach artwork in normative and responsive museum assemblages, they display a tendency to draw on the didactic information presented alongside the works in order to derive meaning. Eyes glance at the artwork, quickly shifting to read the wall text or pamphlet before returning the gaze to the work. If the work is thought to be 'important', the returned gaze is accompanied by increased consideration. At Mona, the absence of traditional sources of information leads visitors to have an extended aesthetic encounter, relying on their own response to the work to decide whether they wish to engage further by utilising the 'O'. Visitors can choose whether they want aesthetic experiences, or a more traditional pedagogy, to govern their interactions in the exhibition. The 'O' is a crucial resource in the Mona assemblage, as it heightens the capacity for relational interactions, and by extension, the capacity for components to affect back on the assemblage.

The potential of the 'O' is determined by the multitude of layers in its design and how far the subject wishes to explore this particular digital environment. Interaction is dependent on the subjects' familiarity with the affordances of the interface, alongside their preferred narrative creation. The content layer of the 'O' is highly structured, with the overarching categories introduced earlier in this chapter. 'Gonzo' is a particularly interesting addition to the informational layer of the 'O' because it is a reminder of a connecting theme and progression in narrative, which is the unifying constituent that is owner/collector David Walsh. 'Ideas', on the other hand, reinforces the notion of the discontinuity and particularity of narrative. Offering quotes and discussion points that vary between devices encourages a meaning making process that, before becoming dialogical, ask the visitor to relate the 'idea' with the object through a connecting narrative in a way that correlates information and experience. This can be understood through the lens of 'non sequitur' reading. In fact, many of the resources of Mona can be understood as having this same non-sequitur capacity, uncovering a complex system of potential and possibility for both the visitor experience and curatorial strategies.

Architecture

Mona's architecture is also understood as an interface with a non-sequitur layout. It does not lend itself to a linear journey through the exhibition space. It has dead ends, tunnels that lead you somewhere unexpected, narrow rooms, peek-holes, a staircase that diverts to span multiple levels, and a generally haphazard, individualised walking path. With the recent development of further underground tunnels,[8] Mona has reinforced its 'labyrinth' feel. This makes the movement patterns of visitors less predictable to normative museums, whose galleries are usually laid out with a clear path in mind. In my own experience of Mona, the affective practices and interactions were emphasised in the synergy between architecture and atmosphere. Though a large proportion of the art is visual (only a small number of the installations are immersive in the sense that they are 'touchable'), I would argue that, at Mona, we engage the 'haptic eye' which, as Hillier states, is when 'optic becomes tactile' and there is no 'sensory subordination' (Hillier 2012: 140).

At Mona, the material role of the architecture interacts with the expressive role of curatorial strategies (displays that merge antiquities with contemporary art, sound works reverberating off the sandstone, and multiple – sometimes conflicting – narratives). Together, these disrupt the pre-existing 'logic' of museum organisation. Elucidating this interaction between art and architecture, James Pearce[9] has expressed that a conscious decision was made to avoid creating a neutral space for the display of art. Instead, Mona was built with flexibility and adaptability in mind, allowing it to grow and change over time (Pearce Interview, Mona: Architecture n.d.). The capacity for visitors to make their own 'desire lines' (de Certeau 1980) through the exhibition space can be seen as democratising the visitor experience. Alternatively, it can be intimidating. In Karin Harrasser's (2015: 383) research, more autonomous decision-making in exhibition spaces has been found to be an anxiety-inducing experience. Uncertainty in how to navigate space and social behaviours can limit visitor engagement and interaction. Many visitors struggle with the freer format of Mona. A common refrain here is the fear of an incomplete experience. For Walsh and his curators, 'getting lost' in the Mona labyrinth was integral to the visitor experience, encouraging exploration, curiosity and serendipity. Over time, certain compromises have been made. For instance, while Mona was once adamant about only relying on the 'O' for locative measures, visitor guides with maps are now available upon museum entry, and you can now access a map on the 'O' itself. Holzner (2022) reflects on the introduction of a map component, stating:

> I think at some level, Mona is accepting that the original idea of just wanting everyone to be as lost as possible at all times has to be offset with the utility of knowing where the bathrooms are, where exhibition a vs. exhibition b is. It's also due to the physical footprint of the museum. In 2011, it was a lot smaller than what it is now. The museum has grown, probably at least double. As the gallery footprint has ever increased in size, there has been a need to provide some level of wayfinding. If you took an extreme viewpoint, you could say that we should continue to make sure everyone stays lost. That's some of the founding sentiment from David Walsh, he wants you to be caught in the moment, and to not worry about where you are going or the pathway from A to B. The idea is entirely led by our human interest and your personal curiosity. And when Mona is at its best, that holds true and you're in the moment. The map brings you back into the cognitive mindset as opposed to the emotional. But we just have to acknowledge that being lost all the time is frustrating, you don't want to have a certain percentage of the audience frustrated because they can't find a bathroom. Another reason for the map being introduced is that you have all these specific paid works and specific commissions. . . . Mona evolves over time, like all institutions, and things change as a result of that.

The introduction of a map component can be seen as a result of the visitor assemblage interacting with the wider Mona assemblage in a way that affirms the strength of the normative common notion. It is an indication that visitors to museums have come to expect the more structured experiences of normative assemblages. The characteristic of flexibility – found within Pearce's statement and the emergent common notion – is partially disrupted by both the visitor guide and more permanent art installations. It sheds light on how institutionalisation is partially fuelled by pragmatism, the needs of the visitor component, and the growth of the museum.

Collections

Much of Mona's collection and display references the theatricality, private ownership, anachronistic display, personal narrative, and the elements of fetishist object collection aligned with practices found in the *Wunderkammer*, or curiosity cabinet. This serves to bolster Stephen Bann's claim that 'we are now experiencing a kind of historical *ricorso* to curiosity' (Bann 2008: 117). An example of the anachronistic mode of display at Mona is found in the death chamber of Pausiris, which contains both an Egyptian mummy from the Ptolemaic to Roman Period (100BCE to 100CE) and a Serrano photograph *The Morgue (Blood Transfusion Resulting in AIDS)* (1992). The visitor, interacting with this space, is encouraged to imagine the connections between these works. This also invokes the pansemiotic tradition of the *Wunderkammer* (Westerhoff 2001). In the *Wunderkammer*, pansemioticism allowed for one object to signify a variety of meanings for the collector, with the expectation that enough objects with multiple significations would lead to a universal collection. In this way, we could consider Mona to be Walsh's personal memory archive, an interplay of the singular vision of the collector and the pansemioticism in the relationship between the collector and the object. However, as Mona is a museum open to the public, Walsh is not the only human component to enter into this assemblage. As such, the potential flexibility of meaning is heightened. Rather than take the normative museum approach, through which the ordering and display of works is underpinned by an Enlightenment rationale, Mona establishes a link of continuity with Renaissance-inspired pansemiotics.

Former Mona curator Nicole Durling has previously stated that the individual works within the collection are judged in terms of how Walsh interacts with the piece and whether it gives a different sensation to the experience. The emphasis on sensation and individual meaning-making invokes the practices of affective museums more broadly (see Chapter 5). Rather than playing to a universal objectivity, Mona is self-reflexively subjective:

> Many galleries, as you probably already know, present themselves as a neutral space in which the goal is to let the art shine with as little distraction and interference as possible. We respect this, not least because it gives us a point of difference, and allows us to be exclusive – in the sense that not all peoples, times and places are represented in our collection, as they are, and should be, in public institutions.
>
> (Mona: Introduction n.d.)

The implications of this include the renegotiation of cultural authority and the establishment of cultural capital outside of traditional institutions. As we saw in 'priorities', the building and the technology in Mona are considered equal in value to the artwork by Walsh and the Mona staff. This destabilisation of hierarchy within the museum is a move away from the normative practices that encourage a perception of the collection as the central feature of both museum operations and visitor experience.

Mona deliberately plays with the private–public nature of the museum. In 2022, the lowest level of the museum, just hidden from view off to the side of the Void Bar, had been turned into an intimate music venue reminiscent of the speakeasy, complete with moody lighting, seating to sink into, and a small stage framed by ruched red curtains with a gold fringe trim. The stage is presented as a miniature studio, currently home to one of Mona's musicians-in-residence, Ben Salter, who performs his work interspersed with cynical musings. The floor is carpeted with a dramatic purple, red, and gold pattern that wouldn't be out of place in a Vegas casino. Large circular coffee tables surrounding by seating emit a faint glow. Closer inspection of one of the tables shows artwork by Gregory Green – in the form of representational sculptures of terrorist paraphernalia – installed inside. The other is home to Stephen J Shanabrook's *Morgue Series: New York* (2000–2005), chocolate sculptures of wounds collected from dead bodies in a New York morgue. Along one of the walls of the long, rectangular room, the deep red curtain continues. A photograph *India (Frost)* (2013) by Ryan McGinley and a painting *The Arse End of the World* (1994) by Juan Davila hang side by side. A mirror separates these from an etching by Goya, part of his *Los Desastres de la Guerra* series (1810–1820) and a thickly framed Renoir *Jeune femme se baignant* (1888). Each work depicts variations of the nude form – male, female, beautiful, grotesque, mutilated, politicised, worshipped, objectified. Works acquired from the Picasso-designed ceramic and earthenware collections are housed in one of Mona's many cabinets, alongside volumes of books and the occasional framed image. On the wall opposite, small windows at eye level spotlight pocket-sized objects, providing peepholes into figurines and amulets from Egyptian antiquity, as well as a skinned kitten trophy rug (2005) by Julia deVille.

Early on, in reference to Mona, David Walsh said to media, 'I don't care if it all burns down or washes away', shifting the purpose away from this traditional education/conservation dynamic and into a present reality that deals with immediacy, entertainment, and obsolescence. Now, with the new tunnel extensions and their large-scale art installations, the spatio-temporality of the assemblage is extended. Walsh writes: 'While planning and populating [the tunnel extension] Pharos, I saw it as many, often contradictory, things. It is a counterpoint to Mona, a changeless thing, a legacy and a totem' (Walsh 2018a). The Mona collection as temporary and dynamic is now conceived as more permanent. Works in the tunnel chambers are site-specific, and their materiality does not afford the same flexible capacity of the other *Monanisms*. For the most part, *Monanisms* works are taken down and exhibitions altered relatively spontaneously, with a playful 'let's see how this goes' attitude that often results in a trial and error process.

Professional Staff

Though the assemblage is reliant on all component interactions, we have seen the importance of individuals in the directives of museums throughout each assemblage. In the private museum, the collector plays a heightened role, as it is through them that the museum's objects and artworks are amassed. All staff agree that Walsh is extremely involved with what happens at the museum, though this does not mean it is a one-man operation. Mona's website notes: 'Most of what we do at Mona is dear to David's heart, but sometimes he is happy to stand back and see what his team comes up with. Even so, we live in fear of God' (Mona: Introduction n.d.). Mona is unusual for bringing in staff who are not considered museum experts. This is crucial, as museum experts share a habitus that helps affirm a common notion. Thus, by bringing in people from 'outside' this field, the assemblage may be deterritorialised. According to Pearce (2015), Walsh was more concerned with whether his team would 'challenge him in productive ways' and would be prepared to question the ways things are normatively done. Pearce herself was hired to write content for Mona and act as a 'kind of in-house art critic', despite having no marketing experience or art background. Nonetheless, some more normative processes are now discernible. Over the years, with the museum's growth and the introduction of additional paid experiences in the museum space, gallery invigilators play a much more active role in instructing and directing visitors. Previously, the gallery floor staff would territorialise the objective of keeping visitors 'lost' and would encourage self-direction.

Mona's Publics

We cannot understand Mona's 'publics' unless we first acknowledge that the experience of Mona exists in a multi-sited realm, both physical and virtual. This is not unique to Mona. As Lynda Kelly states, 'museums now operate across three spheres: Their physical site, the online world (via websites and social media) and in the mobile space' (2013: 54). Across each of my Mona visitations, overhearing numerous visitors compare the reality of their visit with their expectations is evidence of the attention Mona has received from media. Combined with the prevalence of the Mona brand through word-of-mouth, across social networking services and through the Mona weblog and website, the 'rumour' of Mona precedes the visitor experience on site. Wandering around Mona, one hears numerous assertions that highlight the role of rumour for reinforcing or disrupting the visitor expectation of Mona. One visitor, looking at Nolan's rainbow serpent, exclaims 'Oh, I love this! I saw a photo of it'. Another turns to a friend and says 'Nothing blew me away. I was expecting the vagina wall, or the toilet to, but they didn't'.[10] Mona cannot exist outside of the relational interactions that visitors bring to the space, which to a degree are based on their relational interactions prior to Mona.

Ongoing conversation around the museum is evident on its social media sites, most notably Instagram and Facebook. For Glynda Hull and John Scott, an idealised outcome of interaction on a social media site is to 'prompt users to imagine meaning beyond their own immediate reactionary perspective' (Hull and Scott 2013: 135). Through networked sites like Facebook, which attach identities to commentary (through a reasonably well-observed real-name policy), Mona relates to individuals, and individuals relate to Mona – as well as to each other – in a way that negotiates the meaning, purpose, and role of the institution. The use of slang and anecdotal references proliferates its marketing material as well as on-site communication. The casual tonality on Mona's Facebook feed is not only a reflection of the medium but a reflection of the successful understanding of the visitor's desire to be spoken to like a 'friend' of Mona. The concept of conviviality, explored later in the emergent assemblage (see Chapter 6), plays an essential role in how we understand the interactions explored in this section. In many forms of governance, from government to corporate, the potential unruliness of conviviality is mitigated as part of the control and containment strategies of museums. Conviviality, on the other hand, is openness made manifest. As such, Mona's governance takes shape through conviviality rather than forging against it.

Mona not only utilises online platforms to communicate *to* but also to communicate *with* its publics. Museums and museum scholars alike have increasingly turned to the potential of museums' virtual communities, for the purposes of marketing reach, access, and strengthening community engagement. Most museums tend to utilise these technologies in order to publicise events and release promotional or informative material, rather than to create a dialogue between visitors and museum professionals (Dewdney et al. 2013). We see a distinct one-way communication across these platforms that aligns with the normative practices of pedagogy, museum authority, and controlled environments. Mona, on the other hand, has comment functions enabled across all of its networking sites, allowing visitors and potential visitors to respond to Mona's content and to each other.

We see this in effect when we look at engagement on the Mona blog. Often posts are written by Walsh, and reader comments infer a kind of familiarity with the collector, with the majority of comments directed towards 'David' or the more acquainted 'Walshie'. When Walsh wrote an entry for the Mona weblog that detailed his daughter's hospital visit, it was met with an outpouring of condolences and well-wishing from not only acquaintances of Walsh but also numerous strangers who had connected to the weblog because they had visited or were planning on visiting the museum. The amount of commentary on the weblog entry led Walsh to publishing a response to his respondents, which largely addressed ideas on religion, death, and the nature of chance, themes which are featured prominently through the works displayed in Mona.

What can be observed in the above anecdote is the crucial role Walsh plays in the public's imagination of Mona. The public connects with, or at the very least wishes to understand, the mind behind the museum: 'People always want to know more about David. That's tough, because this whole enterprise is an expression of his character – or, more accurately, an attempt for him to get to know himself better' (Mona: Introduction n.d.). That visitors can communicate with Walsh in the online realm furthers this sense of connection and fascination. Hull and Scott note that 'Museums have traditionally focused curatorial efforts on the romanticized notion of the author/artist and the artifacts of his creation' (2013: 137). In Mona, this focus can be interpreted as having shifted from the 'lone creative genius' figure of the artist, to the eccentric figure of Walsh. That the visitor responds to Mona as a personification of Walsh is affirmed by the curatorial practices and branding strategies employed by the museum. We see this in the popularity of the 'Gonzo' content, the written component of Walsh's personal narrative, which remains the most popular piece of content in terms of access (Holzner 2022) and in terms of what visitors speak about (Pearce 2013b).

On the Mona blog we see a high level of engagement, with some blog posts having hundreds of comments. Walsh explicitly invites dialogue. For instance, when reflecting on a controversial decision to invite a performance piece by artist Hermann Nitsch, Walsh ends his post with 'I expect more than the usual number of responses to this tirade. I do hope I learn something' (Walsh 2018b). In Ned Rossiter's exploration of networks, he writes that in institutional frameworks knowledge is contained in such a way that it both 'refuses the social relations that make possible the development of intellectual action' and 'refutes the potential for social transformation' (2006: 96). Through the consistent engagement with visitors to the Mona blog, knowledge is set free, forging social relations. What is important, beyond the comments by readers, is that Walsh responds to some of these comments, effectively establishing a dialogue. Critical and sometimes downright insulting comments are not filtered or deleted in an administrative process. Rather, they are kept as part of the ecology of debate generated by both the proposed event and Walsh's musings on it. There have certainly been moments where Mona has alienated communities, leading to extensive criticism.

In June of 2014, for the exhibition *Southdale Shopping Centre*, the entrance and foyer of Mona was temporarily reimagined to look like a mall, and part of the basement level transformed into the 'C'MONA Community Centre'. During this exhibition, one of many installations in Mona's foyer was a display offering free (but faux) genetic DNA testing and the question 'are you of Aboriginal descent?' While intended as satirical, there was a backlash from members of the Tasmanian Aboriginal community who rightly claimed it was reminiscent of the objectification and othering of Australian Aboriginals and their culture in former museum exhibitions elsewhere. Consequently, Walsh released an apology on the Mona blog and removed the DNA display. Mona reacted in a way that did not align with the priorities of 'controversy' and 'not being dictated to' that were expressed through its brand values. Instead, we saw a full apology statement issued. This was the first – but not the last – time we saw, publicly, Mona being divided in its loyalty to an artist (the stand was part of the wider exhibition devised by Büchel), and responsibility to its public and community. While Walsh immediately removed the offending piece, this was not taken well by Büchel, who felt it compromised the integrity of his work. This event calls into question the role of the museum and the nature of the communities it serves, showing that even though Mona prides itself on being controversial, it is not exempt when taking issues of cultural heritage (tangible and intangible) into question.[11] The 'move fast and break things' mentality of Mona can, at times, be at odds with its growing responsibility to its publics.

Many of the practices explored here can be read through the lens of Chantal Mouffe's 'agonistic pluralism', which transforms one of the perceived cornerstones of democracy, participation, into occupation (Mouffe 2013: 26). Occupation in this context is defined by El Baroni as 'the aspiration to occupy institutional frameworks through the radicalization of the democracy' (El Baroni 2017: 231). We see this aspiration manifest in Mona's claims towards anti-authority, its playfulness in embracing institutional forms in order to subvert them, as well as its collaborations with local/state governing bodies and established curators alongside various affordances for the visitor in their capacity to act. The communicative practices outlined above are confirmations of dialogue between Mona and its publics. Though at times disruptive and antagonistic, these are viewed as productive forces. This indicates a self-reflexive perspective that acknowledges Mona as an assemblage in flux.

Self-determination

In priorities, I noted that the aim of 'pedagogy and pleasure' formed an ambiguous hybridity in the visitor experience of Mona. Mona accommodates a range of modalities and subjectivities that ultimately afford visitors more choice in how they experience the museum. This is supported by a large-scale Mona visitor experience survey, in which 87% (n. 5576) of respondents said that compared to other museums, they felt freer to choose their experience of art (Franklin and Papastergiadis 2017: 680). Here, we can take Natalia Radywyl's (2008) analysis of 'self-determination'[12] within museum visitor experience and extend it to consider self-determination as an indicator of an increased capacity to affect within an assemblage. Harrasser positions this within a wider context of museum practice claiming that the social democratic idea of education for all is mixed with entertainment, creating a hybrid of 'participatory approaches' with 'pure consumer optimism' (2015: 385). As a result of this hybridity, the visitor to Mona takes on many different modalities through their experience: a consumer at the Void Bar, active participants engaging with haptic artworks, users of the 'O', audiences at the Mona cinema, companions socially bonding, spectators in art-worshipful contemplation, and so on.

The 'O' device further compounds these multiple modalities. As is stated on the Mona website, 'We believe things like art history and the individual artist's intention are interesting and important – but only alongside other voices and approaches that remind us that art, after all, is made and consumed by real, complex people – whose motives mostly are obscure, even to themselves' (Mona: Introduction n.d.). When asked how Mona makes space for multiple subjectivities, Elizabeth Pearce stated:

> We show our human flaws. This is apparent on our O device, the mobile guide patrons take with them as they move through the gallery, and that delivers a range of different interpretation and commentary on the art. We always wanted to present Mona as multi-vocal: if we air our flaws, biases and contradictions, the audience will find a space to do the same, and therefore have a more meaningful engagement with the art, one that involves their whole selves and that they can take away with them to the wider world.
>
> (Pearce 2015)

However, many visitors struggle with this flattening of hierarchy at Mona. This serves to indicate the ways in which the normative modality of visitor as art-worshipful spectator has been internalised. In Mona the visitor is asked to relearn the way they experience a museum. Nonetheless, one can choose to assume the role of art historian, by engaging with 'Artwank', or become a friend to Walsh by engaging with 'Gonzo'. Within the exhibition *On the Origin of Art* (2017), an audio accompaniment on the 'O' relayed the divergent perspectives of four curators, each given an exhibition space to explore the relationship between art and biology. These multiplicities accommodate a variety of subjectivities that encourage visitors to construct their own narrative through their interactions, and question the notion of a singular, authoritative voice. We see that self-determination is also evident in visitor movement and in turn, navigation through the space is different every visitation.

The potentiality of self-determination is impacted by a visitor's ability to interpret the way in which components come together in a space. Visitors are quick to interpret the cues of spatial layout. In the rooms curated with a more normative layout (art in vitrines, sculptural pieces in the centre), Mona visitors reverted to walking through in a normative and prescribed manner. This was the case with the *River of Fundament* (2015) exhibition. Visitors first moved around the walls to look at the hung works, before moving into the centre to the sculptural pieces. I observed visitors engaging in 'interaction order' (Goffman 1983), following the movement patterns of other visitors within the space and waiting in turn for each artwork. Within *Monanisms*, without normative spatial 'cues', visitor movement is more free-form.

In the temporary exhibition *River of Fundament*, normative walking patterns highlight the idea that component relations within a space prompt a set of relations and can be naturalised over time (thus solidifying an assemblage). When borrowed – as they are in a temporary exhibition – they become signifiers and social cues for a spatially and culturally literate visitor body, rather than a re-territorialisation of the assemblage. While visitors reverted to normative movement within *River of Fundament*, this did not eradicate self-determination, due to the continued affordance of multiple subjectivities. Art is interpreted aesthetically and conceptually, embodied experiences impact on the visitor experience, and there is room for individual choices in engagement. Components have relations of exteriority. As Andrea Fraser states, 'Many visitors are unable to challenge the boundaries that are set for them by their life experience. Their own frame restricts the discourse available to them to make meaning' (Fraser 2005: 298). The hybridity of Mona not only influences but accommodates the meaning-making processes of visitors. Multiple visitor modalities and subjectivities lend themselves to self-determined participation. No singular account could support the variety of visitor experiences of Mona, and visitor engagement with Mona should be understood as layered, rather than hierarchical.

Mona's Processes

Mona has been seen to exhibit characteristics perceived as anomalies to existing ideas of what a museum is, and what we expect from them. Adrian Franklin describes Mona as an 'anti-museum' (2014, 2019), stating that 'Except for showing art, MONA pretty much reversed the modus operandi of conventional museums' (2014: 87). He continues:

> MONA changed the museum environment itself: not just its architecture and interior, but its ambience, its warmth and humanity, its accessibility, its allure, its purpose, its delivery– and, critically, its dependence on the wall label.
>
> (Franklin 2014: 87)

While Franklin's argument is relevant, it arises from a base of comparison with the normative museum. Museums that display interactions aligned with the emergent museum assemblage tend to be seen as antithetical to the traditional idea of what constitutes a museum. The anti-museum is a term used to denote the component interactions that deviate from the normative (Copeland and Lovay

2017). Mona is indeed deviant if we are to follow the typological tradition that positions museum practice in relation to the 'white cube' model. If we position Mona within an assemblage approach, which illustrates a variety of different practices making up the museum, a more tangled picture emerges. Mona can be better understood as a 'singular haecceity', which includes the network of connections that draw from the long history of museum development. In relation to the historical genealogy and institutional critique, there are multiple threads of continuity and points of convergence that demonstrate Mona is in conversation with this history. Mona as an assemblage in relation to the four common notions explored in this work, further complicates these interwoven connections.

What we find through the processes of Mona is twofold. First, we find expressions of visitor agency that show an empowered perception of their capacity to affect within the assemblage, which aligns with emergent museum practices. Second, we see a shift in Mona's practices that see it oscillating between assemblages, creating fascinating contradictions in its practices. These insights into the priorities, resources and publics that make up Mona's processes suggest a self-reflexivity, a role in community-building, and a dynamism inherent to its structure. The latter suggests an ability to respond with a swiftness that mirrors the compression of time and space emblematic to our current era.

No museum is immune from other assemblage's capacity to affect. What has struck me, over my seven-plus years of observing Mona, is its progression towards institutionalism. With Mona's success comes the desire to link it to governmental assemblages, to tourism and policies, and to museum practices such as conservation and permanency. As we saw, Walsh initially thought he would be happy to sit and watch the artworks 'rot' if no one came to the museum, though he later acknowledges that he does care about their preservation. As the museum has grown (in exhibition space, collection, and sense of community ownership), Walsh has reassessed his stance in relation to visitor needs and desires. Formally holding a self-confessed dismissive attitude, he has since stated that the relationship between Mona and its community is important, and that this has led him to care more about the 'legacy' of Mona.

Professional staff at Mona are well aware of the shift towards institutionalisation the museum is experiencing. Leigh Carmichael has stated that although they started as the 'anti-establishment', they are 'unfortunately' now the establishment (Coslovich 2018). Likewise, Walsh has stated that he is 'concerned about the push to the centre. . . . I certainly don't want to be the MCA or the Tate Modern' (Coslovich 2018). Pearce (2015) notes that, over time, their once 'teen-rebellion attitude' has shifted to one of 'community responsibility', leading to tensions between retaining their 'authentic edge' whilst respecting their audiences. Mona, as a private museum, did not initially have to become part of a 'governmentalized public culture' (Witcomb 2003: 101), and it does not rely on government funding to survive. Because of its trajectory, even when it does collaborate with government, Mona has more power within the relationship to make demands.

As Mona moves forward in time, coming into prolonged contact with governmental and social assemblage systems, it will be interesting to see whether the 'charismatic leadership' (Weber 1947; DeLanda 2006) of Walsh allows Mona to retain its dynamic nature. We have already seen many instances where a more solid mission of what Mona is and should be emerge, predominantly in relation to ideas around its role in the community. This serves to highlight the multidirectional way in which components of a museum interact and invoke different assemblages. Paradoxically, Mona's point of consistency is its contradictory nature. Its component relations are still in overt processes of negotiation. If we relationally position Mona's practices to the practices of the other museums explored in this book, we see how rapidly Mona draws on practices that are of the normative, responsive, affective, and emergent common notions. For the time being, this constant flux positions it within the emergent museum assemblage.

Through an assemblage systems lens, our understanding of museum practice can be developed. In turn, the analysis of Mona becomes an exercise in understanding the processes of 'fleeing, instituting and transforming' (Raunig 2009: 3). Instead of the claustrophobic grip of neat narratives, this embraces complexity, tension, experimentation, and potential. Mona displays a complexity of practices that, at times, are indicative of one or more of each of the museum assemblages. This serves to problematise the claims towards Mona's uniqueness, while still looking at the productive effects of its practices. We can place the emphasis on the museum's dynamism and potentiality, rather than purely documenting a museum within a singular typology or emphasising some practices over others in order to paint a picture of Mona as 'the next step' in a historical trajectory. This means that, instead of approaching Mona from an ideology of 'progression' (in relation to a historical trajectory), we can analyse the multi-dimensional processes of its (constant) becoming. This moves the research away from the 'hype' surrounding Mona, instead framing it as part of a broader context of museum practices by looking towards other museums around the globe. By examining museological accounts and empirically cross-checking them within contemporary museum practice, we find a far more complex interplay than an assumption of change and continuity as binary oppositions. Even through a brief overview of Mona, we see that it exceeds existing museum typologies. Increasingly, cultural institutions are mirroring the dynamism we have explored through Mona's practices. This indicates a need for an analytical lens that is as dynamic as the institutions it aims to unpack.

Notes

1 This framework is borrowed from Conal McCarthy's (2015) overview of museum practice.
2 Mona's collection catalogue.
3 By 2019, the Mona 'brand' was comprised of 40 different creative ventures.
4 Originally the brand designer for Moorilla Estate, later (from 2013 to 2023) the Creative Director of Dark Mofo, the midwinter arts and music festival hosted by Mona.

5 The visitor survey (conducted in 2014 as part of the ARC project *Creating the Bilbao effect: MONA and the social and cultural coordinated of urban regeneration through arts tourism*) of Mona showed that 73% of Mona's visitors are tertiary educated, 30% of that with a post-graduate level qualification. The majority indicated a high level of cultural capital (Measured by the individual's collective gallery and museum visitation over the 12 months preceding the Mona survey).
6 Through the combination of wireless sensors and Radio Frequency Identification (RFID) tags situated throughout the museum, the 'O' is able to push location-based content to the visitor through the app.
7 Situated in a wider context shows that this consideration is neither stance nor chance; specific affordances relating to geolocation technologies were maturing at the time of Mona's construction.
8 In December 2017 the 'Pharos' wing opened, which leads you from underground to jutting out over the River Derwent. In 2019 the Siloam extension (a series of tunnels and chambers) opened, connecting Pharos to Mona's original underground exhibition space. In the same year, Mona opened the immersive experience *The Divine Comedy* by artist Alfredo Jaar.
9 Director of Architecture for Fender Katsalidis.
10 Mona visitation notes, January 22, 2017.
11 Mona has since had other controversies, most notably in 2021, due to an artwork titled *Union Jack* by Santiago Sierra, which called for First Nations Peoples to donate blood, which would then be used by Sierra to soak a British flag. Apologies were once more issued, and the artwork was pulled.
12 Based on Beck and Beck-Gernsheim's (2003) concepts of individualisation and agency within the wider framework of reflexive modernity.

References

Bann, Steven (2008). 'The Return to Curiosity: Shifting Paradigms in Contemporary Museum Display'. A. McClellen (ed.) *Art and its Publics: Museum Studies at the Millennium*. Oxford: Blackwell Publishing Ltd. Pp. 117–130.
Beck, Ulrich and Elisabeth Beck-Gernsheim (2003). 'Losing the Traditional: Individualization and "Precarious Freedoms"'. *Individualization: Institutionalized Individualism and Its Social and Political Consequences*. London/California/New Delhi: Sage. Pp. 1–21.
Booth, Kate, Justin O'Connor, Adrian Franklin and Nikos Papastergiadis (2017). 'It's a Museum, But Not as We Know It: Issues for Local Residents Accessing the Museum of Old and New Art'. *Visitor Studies* 20(1). Pp. 10–32.
Carvalho, Lucila (2017). 'The O in MONA: Reshaping Museum Spaces'. L. Carvalho, P. Goodyear and M. de Laat (eds.) *Place-Based Spaces for Networked Learning*. New York/Oxon: Routledge.
Copeland, Mathieu and Balthazar Lovay (2017). *The Anti-Museum: An Anthology*. London: Fri-Art and Koenig Books.
Coslovich, Gabriella (2018). 'Tasmania's Dark Mofo Gets Darker as MONA Influence Expands'. *The Australian Financial Review Magazine*, 23 February 2018. https://www.afr.com/afrmagazine/tasmanias-dark-mofo-gets-darker-asmona-influence-expands-20180117, last accessed 26 January 2022.
Davila, Juan. (1994). *The Arse End of the World*. Museum of Old and New Art, Hobart, Tasmania. Painting. Oil and collage on canvas.
De Certeau, Michel (1980). *The Practice of Everyday Life*. S.F. Rendall (trans.) (1984). Berkeley/Los Angeles/London: University of California Press.

DeLanda, Manuel (2006). *A New Philosophy of Society: Assemblage Theory and Social Complexity*. London/New York: Continuum.

DeVille, Julia. (2005). *Kitten Trophy Rug*. Museum of Old and New Art, Hobart, Tasmania. Kitten pelt with metallic kid leather backing, glass eyes, diamonds and akoya pearl.

Dewdney, Andrew, David Dibosa and Victoria Walsh (2013). *Post Critical Museology: Theory and Practice in the Art Museum*. London/New York: Routledge.

El Baroni, Bassam. (2017). 'The Post-Agonistic Institution: Four Positions on the Structural Relation between Art and Democracy'. Paul O'Neill, Lucy Steeds, and Mick Wilson (eds.) *How Institutions Think: Between Contemporary Art and Curatorial Discourse*. Cambridge MA: MIT Press. Pp. 229–235.

Falk, John, Lynn D. Dierking, and Marianna Adams. (2006). 'Living in a Learning Society: Museums and Free-choice Learning'. Sharon MacDonald (ed.) *A Companion to Museum Studies*. Malden, MA/ Oxford/ Victoria: Blackwell Publishing. Pp. 323–339.

Franklin, Adrian (2014). *The Making of MONA*. UK: Penguin.

Franklin, Adrian (2019). *Anti-Museum*. London/New York: Routledge.

Franklin, Adrian and Nikos Papastergiadis (2017). 'Engaging with the Anti-Museum? Visitors to the Museum of Old and New Art'. *Journal of Sociology* 53(3). Pp. 670–686.

Fraser, Andrea (2005). 'From the Critique of Institutions to an Institution of Critique'. *Artforum* 44. Pp. 278–283.

Goffman, Erving (1983). 'The Interaction Order: American Sociological Association, 1982 Presidential Address'. *American Sociological Review* 48(1). Pp. 1–17.

Goya, Francisco. (1810–1820). *Esto es peor*. Plate 37 of *Los Desastres de la Guerra* (The Disasters of War). Museum of Old and New Art, Hobart, Tasmania. Print. Etching, lavis, drypoint.

Harrasser, Karin (2015). '(Dis)playing the Museum: Artifacts, Visitors, Embodiment, and Mediality'. M. Henning (ed.) *International Handbook of Museum Studies: Museum Media*. Malden/Oxford: Wiley Blackwell. Pp. 371–388.

Hicks, Megan (2005). '"A Whole New World": The Young Person's Experience of Visiting the Sydney Technological Museum'. *Museum and Society* 3(2). Pp. 66–80.

Hillier, Jean (2012) 'Liquid Spaces of Engagement: Entering the Waves with Antony Gormley and Olafur Eliasson'. *Deleuze Studies* 6(1). Pp. 132–148.

Holzner, Tony (2022). *Interview with Jasmin Pfefferkorn*. Melbourne, 28 November 2022.

Hull, Glynda and John Scott (2013). 'Curating and Creating Online: Identity, Authorship, and Viewing in a Digital Age'. Kirsten Drotner and Kim Christian Schrøder (eds.) *Museum Communication and Social Media: The Connected Museum*. New York/Oxon: Routledge. Pp. 130–149.

Hooper-Greenhill, Eilean (2000). *Museums and Interpretation of Visual Culture*. London: Routledge.

Kelly, Lynda. (2013). 'The Connected Museum in the World of Social Media.' Kristen Drotner and Kim Christian Schrøder (eds.) *Museum Communication and Social Media: The Connected Museum*. New York: Routledge. Pp. 54–71.

Kidd, Jenny (2014). *Museums in the New Mediascape: Transmedia, Participation, Ethics*. Surrey/Burlington: Ashgate Publishing, Ltd.

McCarthy, Conal (ed.) (2015). 'Grounding Museum Studies: Introducing Practice'. *The International Handbooks of Museum Studies: Museum Practice*. Malden/Oxford: Wiley Blackwell. Pp. xxxv–lii.

McGinley, Ryan. (2013). *India (Frost)*. Museum of Old and New Art, Hobart, Tasmania. Photograph. Type-C.

Mona: Introduction (n.d.). https://mona.net.au/museum/introduction, last accessed 18 January 2018.

Monanisms (2010). *Monanisms*, 1st edition. Hobart: Museum of Old and New Art.

Mouffe, Chantal (2013). *Agonistics: Thinking the World Politically*. London and New York: Verso.

On the Origin of Art. (2017). Museum of Old and New Art. Exhibition. Viewed 21 January 2017.

Pearce (Mead), Elizabeth (2013a). 'Preface to the Second Edition'. *Monanisms*, 2nd edition. Hobart: Museum of Old and New Art. Pp. xvi–xvii

Pearce (Mead), Elizabeth (2013b). 'Interview Transcript'. C. Wilson *Pervasive Media in Galleries: Space, Networks, and Transformations*. Masters thesis. School of Culture and Communication, The University of Melbourne.

Pearce, Elizabeth (2015). 'Our Secret'. *Presented to MONA EFFECT 4: Regenerating City and Region through Art Tourism?* Hobart: MONA, 18 September.

Pearce, James (n.d.) 'Mona: Architecture'. https://mona.net.au/museum/architecture, last accessed 11 January 2019.

Radywyl, Natalia (2008). *Moving Images, the Museum and a Politics of Movement: A Study of the Museum Visitor*. Doctoral dissertation, University of Melbourne, School of Culture and Communications & School of Historical Studies.

Raunig, Gerald (2009). 'Instituent Practices: Fleeing, Instituting, Transforming'. G. Raunig and G. Ray (eds.) *Art and Contemporary Critical Practice: Reinventing Institutional Critique*. London: MayFlyBooks. Pp. 3–12.

Renoir, Pierre-Auguste. (1888). *Jeune femme se baignant* (Young woman bathing). Private collection. Exhibited at Museum of Old and New Art, Hobart Tasmania. Painting. Oil on canvas. Viewed 10 July 2022.

River of Fundament. (2015). Museum of Old and New Art. Exhibition. Viewed 17 January 2015.

Rossiter, Ned. (2006). 'Organized Networks: Transdisciplinarity and New Institutional Forms'. L. Bang Larsen (ed.) (2014) *Networks: Documents of Contemporary Art*. London: Whitechapel Gallery and MIT. Pp. 95–99.

Serrano, Andres. (1992). *The Morgue (Blood Transfusion Resulting in AIDS)*. Museum of Old and New Art, Hobart, Tasmania. Photograph. Cibachrome.

Shanabrook, Stephen J. (2000–2005). *Morgue Series: New York*. Museum of Old and New Art, Hobart, Tasmania. Sculpture. Chocolate.

Southdale Shopping Centre. (2014). Museum of Old and New Art. Exhibition. Viewed 17 June 2014.

Walsh, David (2013). 'Preface to the Second Edition'. *Monanisms*, 2nd edition. Hobart: Museum of Old and New Art. Pp. xiv–xv.

Walsh, David (2014). *A Bone of Fact*. Australia: Picador.

Walsh, David (2017). 'Rising Tide'. *Mona Blog*, 19 April 2017. https://mona.net.au/blog/2017/04/rising-tide, last accessed 1 August 2017.

Walsh, David (2018a). Instagram @monamuseum. https://www.instagram.com/monamuseum/?hl=en, last accessed 12 January 2018.

Walsh, David (2018b). 'By Chance'. *Mona Blog*, 1 March 2018. https://mona.net.au/blog/2018/03/by-chance, last accessed 1 April 2018.

Weber, Max (1947). *The Theory of Social and Economic Organization*. A.M. Henderson and Talcott (trans.). New York: Parsons.

Westerhoff, Jan C. (2001). 'A World of Signs: Baroque Pansemioticism, the Polyhistor and the Early Modern Wunderkammer'. *Journal of the History of Ideas* 62(4). Pp. 633–650.

Wilson-Barnao, Caroline (2022). *Digital Access and Museums as Platforms*. London/New York: Routledge.

Witcomb, Andrea (2003). *Re-Imagining the Museum: Beyond the Mausoleum*. London/New York: Routledge.

2 Museums as Assemblage
Practice and Potential

Traditional binaries are no longer a viable method of analysis when museums are in collaboration with other institutions, local communities, and each other through the loan of objects, exchange of ideas, and participation in cultural events. Studying museums as a rupture from their Enlightenment legacy implies an institutionally directed process and lacks an acknowledgement of wider systems of interaction. It also invokes a feeling of complete overhaul, which again points to a generalisation and oversimplification of museum operations, as well as results in privileging some institutions, while excluding others. Museums interact and intersect with other bodies and spaces, both creating new conversations and solidifying older roles, which in turn sees a shift in how we see some practices endure, some fade away, and others find new iterations. Museum practices today no longer fit neatly into pre-existing categories or historical trajectories. A more expansive, flexible approach, rather than oppositional rhetoric, is needed to analyse the changing nature of relationships to account for collaboration and contradiction in museum practice. To this end, I have developed an assemblage systems lens for the analysis of museum practice. Assemblage systems theory was first coined by Gilles Deleuze and Felix Guattari, as a brief element of the wider text *Mille Plateaux: Capitalisme et Schizophrénie* in 1980, translated to English in 1987 by Brian Massumi as *A Thousand Plateaus: Capitalism and Schizophrenia*. An assemblage is a 'wide variety of wholes constructed from heterogenous parts' (DeLanda 2006: 3). The use of assemblage systems theory through this work primarily draws on Manuel DeLanda's (2006) extension of Deleuze and Guattari's seminal text.

In many ways, this book follows on from the important work done by Andrea Witcomb (2003) in positioning museum practice as a complex terrain of change and continuity. While Witcomb's work highlights how a variety of museum practices are occurring within different institutions at different times, I am interested in extending this argument to consider how the museum oscillates between different practices. Like Witcomb, I am opposed to predisposing museum practice as contextualised by either fixedness or rupture (2003: 5). I position continuity and change as immanent[1] to one another,

DOI: 10.4324/9781003393719-3

utilising assemblage systems theory to look at the generative conditions of contemporary museum practices. Anything other than a system of interpretation that is fundamentally open to the processes of disassembling and reassembling will constrain an analysis that accounts for negotiated practices in museums.

As a social ontology, assemblage systems theory focuses on the dynamics of the entities being studied. Assemblage systems theory as a method is an attempt to 'imagine more flexible boundaries' (Law 2004: 85). The 'method' in method assemblage is the crafting of these boundaries, which in turn can be seen as a 'making of relations' (Law 2004: 84). The aim of the researcher in this process is to step away from the ontology of knowing and instead look towards the ontology of relating. To do this, we take a museum as an assemblage to be explored in terms of its components and the relations. These interactions inform their practice, which in turn present characteristics that are variable (and present as common notions) depending on the process of their relations. Components allow for assemblages to be qualified, their modes of relation serving as criteria through which the assemblage can be discerned. Further, components hold either material or expressive roles, or a combination of both. Components are human and non-human 'bodies', or 'actors', that make up the assemblage. These hold 'relations of exteriority' (DeLanda 2006) and can be detached and make a component of another assemblage. DeLanda (2006) suggests that assemblage components are self-subsistent, but through exercising their capacity in relations of exteriority, their existence within an assemblage can be analysed, consequently providing a perspective on the assemblage itself. For example, museum objects and artworks are often borrowed or lent between institutions. They move between assemblages. Their inclusion into the assemblage is not what creates the assemblage, but rather highlight the way they mobilise relations.

The material role and the expressive role, as articulated by DeLanda (2006), form two axes that define the variable roles that a component in an assemblage may play. In the museum assemblage, people, interfaces, architecture, and objects in the museum space exercise the material role. The expressive roles are enacted through the habits and formations of the material components and are embodied both linguistically and non-linguistically. This indicates that components do not exercise the same capacity to affect back on the museum as a whole. For example, the visitor of the museum does not exercise the same capacity as the museum curator. Within the museum, the visitor component is in contact with a variety of other components/systems and at each stage is offered a variation on their material/expressive role. In exercising their capacity in a habitual way, the component affirms the common notion of the assemblage. For example, in a museum like the Staatsgalerie Stuttgart (see Chapter 3), the limited directional flow delineated by the architecture links to a chronological hang. As the visitor actualises their role of moving through prescribed pathways within the space, in conjunction with a chronological ordering of display, they are positioned to exercise their capacity in a way that reaffirms the priorities of the whole assemblage. This example also sees the visitors' material role highlighted above their expressive role. A comparable set of relations and processes can be found at the Louvre, the Museum of Modern Art (MoMA), and the National Gallery of Victoria (NGV). The practices of these institutions, and the way these practices delineate the scope (limits and opportunities) for components to exercise their role, aid in their perception as a common notion. In the example provided, this lends itself to the normative. However, when different components interact with different systems, it produces another result. Hence why the assemblage is always in a state of becoming.

A visitor to the Museum of Old and New Art (Mona) is faced with multiple navigational choices, no directional signage, and no wall placards. The deviation from the highly structured approach widens the aforementioned scope in capacity. Consequently, components exercise other sets of relations, and another common notion is formed (in this case, the emergent – see Chapter 6). By exploring the relations between components, we are able to address the potentiality for change that occurs in the outliers – anomalies that have been traditionally overlooked or disregarded in the creation of 'neater' sociological categories. This means that the changes and consistencies found in the assemblage are co-produced by the components making up the museum, rather than solely enacted on components in a hierarchical fashion. In other words, components can affect back on each other, and on the assemblage. The importance of affect in this context cannot be understated. Affect is a change in the capacity of both human and non-human 'bodies', which modulates a body's ability to act (Hickey-Moody 2013). The opportunity to affect other components and therefore the assemblage whole exists in every instance of component relations. In turn, every assemblage has the capacity to affect other assemblage systems. What the above quote highlights is that 'affect' is a productive quality of the assemblage. Because components are in a constant process of interaction and relation, the assemblage is never a fixed entity but always experiencing a process of becoming.

In the course of component relations, there is the potential for a component to either disrupt or reinforce the assemblage whole. Deterritorialisation and territorialisation (Deleuze and Guattari 1987; DeLanda 2006) are a valuable starting point to understand change and continuity in museum practice and the museum's role in society (especially in relation to community, knowledge production, and authenticity). All assemblages are, fundamentally, 'open systems' that interact with other assemblages in ways that can stabilise or destabilise the assemblage. Territorialisation refers to the processes that define both the spatial and nonspatial boundaries of the assemblage. Deterritorialisation occurs in a component of the museum assemblage when the open system of the museum interacts with cultural, political, or economic systems, or when any component of the museum assemblage no longer expresses obedience within the assemblage. These destabilising events can either be routinised (territorialising what could potentially be deterritorialised) or lead to a shift in the nature of the assemblage. Here we find answers for why some museums are perceived as more fixed and others as more dynamic, and why some practices are seen as changing and others as consistent. Without components interacting in a way that aligns with the perception of an assemblage as a (bounded) 'body', the body does not become actualised. These relations are contingent, meaning components can be 'slotted in and out' of different assemblages (the assemblage is considered different due to the difference in component interactions). Therefore, as opposed to preceding the assemblage, the characteristics of coherence and consistency emerge from the assemblage. The interplay between the material and the expressive roles serves to either sharpen the boundaries of an assemblage (territorialisation) or disrupt the assemblage (deterritorialisation).

In the museum assemblage, territorialisation can first be thought of as the historical trajectories that contribute to inherited rituals, processes and practices. It can also, however, be connected to literal 'territorial ties', the connections to geographic place and local communities. It is also an effect of the expressive components – such as policy documents, mission statements, and contractual obligations to stakeholders – that serve to enforce the legitimacy and authority of the assemblage. The deterritorialisation of an assemblage occurs when other systems intersect with the assemblage, modifying, recombining or replacing its components, or the components behave in divergent ways and exercise a capacity at odds with the workings of the assemblage whole. An example of deterritorialisation in the context of museums can be found through the Louvre, which was deterritorialised as a royal residence to become a public museum. Our focus in this work is on common notions (see introduction), which does not see a complete change in perception (the museums we look at remain consistently recognised as museum assemblages). As such, I've chosen to refer to the process of shifting from one common notion to another as 're-territorialisation', not deterritorialisation. In museums, re-territorialisation occurs when influential individuals take over positions of authority with a view to change a museums priorities and processes, if governmental policies surrounding museums are invoked, when social movements gain momentum, resources diminish or increase, and so on. It is important throughout to avoid conflating 'assemblage' and 'common notion'. These are not used interchangeably – the assemblage denotes the *process of becoming*, while the common notion denotes *cultural perception of an assemblage body* (a sense that what was becoming has 'become').

Museum Practice

According to Deleuze (2007), assemblages are 'various combinations of bodies' that nonetheless produce 'whole regimes of signs'. Each museum assemblage is made up components interacting, which I have referred to more generally as 'museum practice'. Inherent to the concept of 'practice' is the idea of habit and repetition, a parallel to the processes of territorialisation that configure and stabilise assemblages. Drawing on Conal McCarthy's (2015) indicators of museum practice provides a useful language in which to group components in a way that is cohesive yet does not attach the conceptual lens of assemblage systems to a singular institution or point in history. While McCarthy separates practice into 'priorities', 'resources', 'publics', and 'processes', I would like to stress that – in order to not compromise the assemblage method – these terms are used to depict the configuration of component relations rather than create predefined categories. In other words, I untangle these components in order to observe how they come together, rather than the other way around.

Priorities refer to policy frameworks, ethical guidelines, and museum management and indicate the strategic direction of museums (McCarthy 2015: xxxvi). 'Priorities' can be understood as 'a collective assemblage of enunciation, of acts and statements' (Deleuze and Guattari 1987: 88). These are located through the expressive role of policy, mission statements, and documents circulated by management levels within the museum. In order to locate priorities, I access and interpret museum mission statements, documents produced by museum management and policy documents pertaining to museums. Looking at museum mission statements taps into a pre-existing area of focus within museum studies literature. A museum's mission and values are seen to 'capture the essence of the museum' (Fleming 2015: 3), playing a pivotal role in projecting the museum's 'identity'. Working within assemblage systems, they are indicative of how a museum wishes to define and project itself as a (bounded) 'whole'.

Resources refer to the collections, objects, materials contained in the museum and correspondingly the curators, collection managers and staff who acquire, research, care for and manage these resources. It also pertains to museum economics, funding models, sponsorship, marketing, and branding. We can understand objects, artworks, and collections as playing a material role in the assemblage. The processes surrounding collections, including planning, care, management, and development, as well as marketing and branding in terms of financial resources, play an expressive role. A key resource explored through each of the following chapters are media forms, from museum websites and social media accounts to interactive screens and geolocative devices. This focus on media is useful, as it highlights the way in which many texts on museums claim that the introduction of digital media into museums is transformative – leading to more 'emergent' relations. I argue that media forms as part of a wider assemblage are only emergent insofar as the rest of the assemblage reinforces the trajectory of emergence. The intersection of digital media as a component within the museum can be equally territorialised as normative, responsive, or affective, depending on its relationship with other components.

The notion of publics operates on a dual level for McCarthy. They are the audiences that the museum addresses and also the products created by the museum that circulate in the public realm. This extends to how communication is 'used, consumed, mediated and responded to by audiences' (McCarthy 2015: xxxvii). This already begins to indicate the interplay of complex and non-linear influences in open system assemblages. For studying organisations using assemblage theory, DeLanda separates 'elements that play an expressive role, that is, those components that express the legitimacy of the authority' from the ones which play 'a material role, those involved in the enforcement of obedience' (2006: 68). Publics play both a material and expressive role by exercising different sets of capacities. DeLanda sees human bodies as holding the foremost material role in social assemblages (2006: 72). If in alignment with the other components of the museum assemblage, publics will territorialise and stabilise the assemblage. If not, they may play a re-territorialising role.

Processes are defined as the development and delivery of the above resources to publics. It includes the development of exhibitions, trends in permanent and temporary museum display, curatorial theory and practice, and the relationship between museum and community. It is through an analysis of processes that we find distinct moments of re-territorialisation and territorialisation, for these processes bridge resources and publics to provide iterations of knowledge production, community-building, and authenticity. DeLanda (2006) notes that expressive behaviour sends signals to the rest of the assemblage about the intention of the organisation, which I connect to priorities. Expressive behaviour then moves into the implementation of strategies, understood here as processes, which connects with the material elements of the assemblage, and can be understood through resources and (traditionally) publics. Self-professed priorities are found in museum mission statements, and usually find performative iterations through museum resources, processes, and publics. A strong legitimation of the assemblage occurs through expressive and material roles in alliance.

Scale

This framework for exploring relations and becoming has been based around the idea that – with the increasingly transitory nature of museum practices – there are several 'indicators' ('practices' Figure 2.1) in which specific practices can be located and utilised to formulate an understanding of the institution as a whole. Each indicator is itself an assemblage, made from components, whose compositional qualities vary across museum types. These form a 'coding role'. Each assemblage is built up from a multitude of components and their relations. As such, the way to approach an analysis of the museum is from left to right, beginning with the relationships between the components that come together within a spatial and temporal scale.

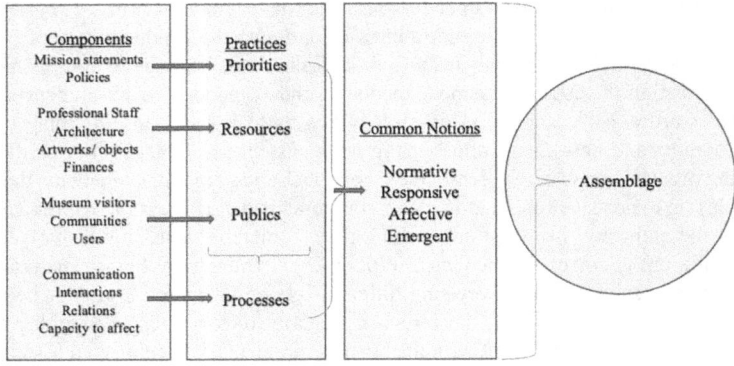

Figure 2.1 Coding Role showcasing scalability from components to assemblage

Scale is key here. According to DeLanda, there are three qualifications for the assemblage system to account for a multi-scaled social reality. The first is the concept of emergence. The second is that networks and organisations come into being as part of a generative processes emerging from other existing assemblages. The third is that particular social processes occur at correspondingly relevant scales (DeLanda 2006: 38–39). The spatial scale posits the whole as larger, in that it is composed of many parts. However, the assemblage also exists a temporal scale. Brian Massumi writes:

> In Deleuze and Guattari, a plateau is reached when circumstances combine to bring an activity to a pitch of intensity that is not automatically dissipated in a climax. The heightening of energies is sustained long enough to leave a kind of afterimage of its dynamism that can be reactivated or injected into other activities, creating a fabric of intensive states between which any number of connecting routes could exist.
>
> (2004: iv)

While change is seen as continuous, a definable assemblage (a singularity) occurs either slowly, as the result of repeated interactions in a cumulative process, or at a more rapid temporality through strategic planning. Strategic planning often involves the mobilisation of internal resources, which prolongs the assemblage duration beyond individual decision-makers. In the museum, legitimacy as an expressive resource plays an integral role to the durability of the museum assemblage. Other resources include material ones, such as funding and professional hierarchies. This highlights the temporal consequences of spatial scales (that they may leave an 'afterimage'). For example, a national museum, which operates on a larger resource scale, would require a greater mobilisation of resources in order to affect change within the assemblage, than a regional museum or smaller scale museum. This is why many national museums assume the normative assemblage, and why we perceive them as slow to change.

The stability of the normative museum assemblage – with its traditional precedents, long-standing entrenched interests, and routinely performed interactions – results in its durability as an assemblage system. Within this spatial and temporal scale, historical significance is considered crucial to the assemblage system. An assemblage body's experience or history is a coordinate for its capacity to affect and be affected. When we look to the museum assemblage, the capacities exercised by a museum through its practices are an extension of their context. It explains, in part, why some institutions are perceived as being 'slow to change' and others appear to respond quickly, and in dynamic ways. No museum is immune to intersections with the political, cultural, economic, and social. However, the way in which museums practice these relations today does not follow a direct and continuous history.

This understanding of spatial and temporal scales is also crucial to understanding the exhibition practices of museums. An overwhelming majority of major museums hold temporary exhibitions, which allow other systems of interaction into the assemblage for a given period of time. These intersections can lead to variable combinations of assemblage – normative museums to hold affective exhibitions, responsive museums to engage in emergent practices, and so on. In the temporary exhibition, components slot in and out of the assemblage, and we see moments of relational interaction, but I argue that these do not change the core characteristics of the assemblage itself, until the components' affect takes a more sustained impact on the museums' practice. It is not until the interactions between assemblage components affect the priorities, resources, processes, and publics of the museum that the assemblage shifts as a common notion. Take, for example, the Louise Bourgeois commission (2000) for the Tate Modern's Turbine Hall, which encouraged visitors to have an embodied experience reminiscent of an emergent or affective museum assemblage. This did not permeate and challenge the other systems in play at the Tate – its priorities, resources, and publics did not shift, rather it was a temporary invocation of a different process, in this case, when the artist component interacted with other systems.

Potential

Assemblage systems theory is based on the principle that the virtual is always actualised through the act of conceiving it. In this work, I give the function of theory a different meaning by applying an assemblage systems methodology to museology. I endeavour to unlock theory from its authoritative and structural foundation, offering it dynamic lines of flight. By repositioning theory as a force that *traces* rather than *captures* complex interactions, I leave space for ambiguity, becoming, and potentiality in museum practice. Through this work, I offer my response to Kylie Message's call to 'write at the edge' (2018). I have operated from the premise that the concept of museums as assemblage is an act of continuous movement, with the inherent potentiality for change in a multitude of directions.

Reframing museums as assemblages to align with the contemporary conditions of museum practice highlights relations, affects, and movements within and between assemblages. These occur across various institutions and through multiple components. Through this, change and continuity are not viewed as binaries, or dualistic pairs, but as holding an immanent relation to one another. George E. Marcus and Erkan Saka (2006: 102) write that while assemblage seems structural, they are instead processes. This problematises the way in which museum studies has previously been approached, as it does not aim towards a recognition of how museums develop, which would rely on pre-existing categories or typologies. Rather, it looks at the conditions that give rise to these new concepts, by analysing the generative potential of the museum as assemblage, something which is continually practiced, affirmed, dismantled, and reassembled.

'Potential' looks at the way in which the lens of assemblage allows us to be open to the destabilizations of neat narratives and wholes. Combined with Kylie Message's (2018) invitation to think critically and self-reflexively about the way in which academics write about museums, I emphasise potentiality in order to embody productive tensions around becoming and dynamism. As Rebecca Coleman and Jessica Ringrose assert, researchers are responding to increasingly complex and entangled areas of study by viewing 'methodology as a relation between what is and what might be' (2013: 7). Without discounting how structural forces are realised – which is fundamental to the way in which museum assemblages are territorialised – my goal is to empower perceptions of agency in component relations.

To pre-emptively address the question of whether a museum can take on the relational interactions of more than one assemblage at a given time, the answer is that they can, and do. However, there is a caveat here. Through my analysis of museums as assemblage systems, I found that the spatial and temporal nature of the assemblage is foundational to understanding the museum as a normative, responsive, affective, or emergent common notion. For example, a common notion is often re-territorialised within temporary exhibitions, but less frequently re-territorialised as a different common notion. Again, we can think of the Bourgeois exhibition at the Tate Modern. While hybridity is rife within present museum practice, the normative, responsive, affective, and emergent common notions represent plateaus – even if the emergent plateau is (paradoxically) only consistent in its self-reflexive and heightened state of inconsistency.

An assemblage is fortified through the relations and perceived capacity of its components. When we look only towards the context of each assemblage, it may appear as though these are historical categories, built as a trajectory from normative to emergent. To dismiss the body-assemblage's experience-history would limit our understanding of affect, and therefore our understand-ing of an assemblage's perceived capacities. However, to focus only on the genealogical contingencies would be to miss a core contention of this work; that the assemblage is alive and always in a state of becoming. This work does not concern itself with progress (linear succession), but process (relational conditions).

I have not sought to create a new set of fixed categories. Rather, the assem-blage is a temporary grouping of relations with constant becoming, and inher-ent potentiality. A museum can take on simultaneous qualities of the normative, responsive, affective, and emergent, showing moments of re-territorialisation and hybridity. The proviso here is that re-territorialisation is only fortified on a spatial and temporal axis. The assemblages I have traced here are expressions of common notions, 'afterimages' that illustrate the multiplicity of museum practice, even as they 'plateau'. In rendering common notions visible (creat-ing the 'afterimage'), several interesting – and sometimes unexpected – con-nections emerged. Normative and responsive museums see overlaps in the interactions between components relating to education and conservation. Affective and emergent museums intersect in through a focus on atmosphere, immersion, as well as drawing on relational aesthetics. The normative and the affective museum assemblages both create spaces for reverence.

Conversely, incongruity also emerged. Responsive and emergent museum assemblages operate on vastly different temporal scales. The former is neces-sarily slow to accommodate community input and the latter is quick in order to react in flexible ways to new interactions. If we take Grant Kester's (2011) work around museums, collaboration, and community we see that responsive-ness, in the sense of a true commitment to communities is, at its heart, a slow process. This leads me to believe that the responsive museum assemblage will likely not be re-territorialised towards an emergent museum assemblage, without losing the interactions that provide the foundations for its responsive-ness. When we incorporate the dynamism of an emergent common notion, the slowness of collaboration is sacrificed. And yet, within both the responsive and the emergent, we see conflict as a productive tension. In the responsive museum conflict is a part of genuinely including constituent voices, while in the emergent museum conflict is inherent to the contradictions that arise from rapid flux.

As a result, I have aimed to avoid placing value judgments on museum practices. For example, 'normative' is not code for 'archaic', it is merely an acknowledgement of repetitive acts and practices with a long spatiotemporal trajectory. I do not see one assemblage as being superior to another. On the contrary, I have come to appreciate their immense value as common notions by looking at their points of intersection. Normative, responsive, affective, and emergent assemblages are comprised of different interactions, which result in different productions of knowledge and community-building, and they all have a role in contemporary society. In the current museum landscape, we have curatorial strategies and visitor experiences that forge an art-worship-ful awe in the normative. In the responsive, these work towards shifting the representation of communities to the presence of communities in the museum. In the affective, we see the privileged position of the sensory and embodied affect. The emergent is a space that accommodates productive contradictions and dynamic practice. Common notions, in relation with one another, illus-trate the multifaceted role of museums and highlight the continued relevance of a diverse array of interactions.

In this, I have engaged with the museum assemblage as a set of circum-stances. The concepts I have developed create new affects and percepts. As Deleuze notes, 'Concepts are inseparable from affects, i.e. from the powerful effects they exert on our life, and percepts, i.e., the new ways of seeing or perceiving they provoke in us' (Deleuze 2007: 238). By honouring the con-cept of potentiality, it is my intention that readers of this work will feel their capacities for affect and imaginative percept enhanced. For museum curators and visitors alike, this reveals how components exercise their capacity in both material and expressive roles. The complexity of these relations situates the components of museums – including, of course, both visitor and curator – in a position where they both affect and are affected. As such, it can be seen as an aide for locating spaces for affect, which may lead to creative, imaginative, and productive enunciations of capacity. For those who study and write on museums, the complexity of potentiality may be daunting, but it is equally liberating, eliciting unexpected connections. Taking a focus on the relational interactions of components welcomes the constant states of negotiation we find in these spaces. In this, it is my hope that scholars taking up the work of analysing museum practices will find value in the critical language I have brought together.

I urge museum scholars to likewise explore museum practice not as an out-come, but as a process. Though I identify the same components in each assem-blage common notion, and use the same language (object, visitor, physical site) to signify them, it is only through the mapping of their relations that the wider assemblage emerges, not through the presence of the components them-selves. The task of this book is to unpack component relations to find how common notions of museum assemblages – that are neither fixed in an histori-cal period (though recognised as having moments of historical significance), nor to a specific institution – are perceived. This is a move away from museum typologies, into the museum as assemblage, creating an ontology that is neither chronological nor place based. Its framework is instead underpinned by a relationality, which serves to accommodate an understanding of the institution as flexible. By locating the relations between components of the museum assemblages, one can create a framework that is not bound chronologically, nor fixed institutionally. In doing so, the assemblage accommodates a range of conceptual constructs, to look at how museum practices were and are in a constant state of mutability. This is crucial for future museological studies. We, as researchers, would ideally operate through a system of analysis that is as reflexive as the cultural conditions that museums negotiate and that we live through individually and collectively.

Note

1 'Immanent' should be read here as the Deleuzian 'immanence', meaning that everything is within, nothing is oppositional (or transcendent), and everything is in a process of becoming through a constant series of relations.

References

Bourgeois, Louise. (2000). *I Do, I Undo, I Redo*. Turbine Hall, Tate Modern, London. Sculpture, installation. Three steel towers, steel spider.

Coleman, Rebecca and Jessica Ringrose (2013). *Deleuze and Research Methodologies*. Edinburgh: Edinburgh University Press.

DeLanda, Manuel (2006). *A New Philosophy of Society: Assemblage Theory and Social Complexity*. London/New York: Continuum.

Deleuze, Giles (2007). 'On Spinoza'. https://deleuzelectures.blogspot.com/2007/02/onspinoza.html, last accessed 7 February 2017.

Deleuze, Gilles and Felix Guattari (1987 [1980]). *A Thousand Plateaus*. B. Massumi (trans.). London: Continuum.

Fleming, David (2015). 'The Essence of the Museum: Mission, Values, Vision'. C. McCarthy (ed.) *The International Handbooks of Museum Studies: Museum Practice*. Malden/Oxford: Wiley Blackwell. Pp. 3–26.

Hickey-Moody, Anna (2013). 'Affect as Method: Feelings, Aesthetics and Affective Pedagogy'. R. Coleman and J. Ringrose (eds.) *Deleuze and Research Methodologies*. Edinburgh: Edinburgh University Press. Pp. 79–95.

Kester, Grant H. (2011). *The One and The Many: Contemporary Collaborative Art in a Global Context*. Durham/London: Duke University Press.

Law, John (2004). *After Method: Mess in Social Science Research*. London/New York: Routledge.

Marcus, George E. and Erkan Saka (2006). 'Assemblage'. *Theory, Culture & Society* 23(2–3). Pp. 101–106.

Massumi, Brian. (2004). 'Translator's Foreword: Notes on the Translation and Acknowledgements'. G. Deleuze and F. Guattari (eds.) [1980] *A Thousand Plateaus*. London: Continuum Books.

McCarthy, Conal (ed.) (2015). 'Grounding Museum Studies: Introducing Practice'. *The International Handbooks of Museum Studies: Museum Practice*. Malden/Oxford: Wiley Blackwell. Pp. xxxv–lii.

Message, Kylie (2018). *The Disobedient Museum: Writing at the Edge*. Oxon/NY: Routledge.

Witcomb, Andrea (2003). *Re-Imagining the Museum: Beyond the Mausoleum*. London/New York: Routledge.

3   The Normative Museum
The Authoritative Voice of the Museum and the Visitor-as-Spectator

The normative common notion positions the museum visitor within a reverent, art-worshipful mode of spectatorship. It is bonded with the notion of 'disciplining' the public and perpetuates the idea of the museum as an authority on culture. A museum assemblage manifesting as normative is extremely familiar to us, invoking priorities and practices that extend back to the late 1800s, when the Louvre first opened to the public. The normative museum was first territorialised when governmental assemblages took precedence over religious assemblages. Aspects of the museum's religious origins and its growth from private collections continue to be evident within the normative museum today. We see this in architectural designs that invoke temples, or mausoleums, in the aura of 'sacredness' within the space, in the continued importance of private donors, and the persistent perception (and sometimes enactment) of elitism.

The display and layout of these museums is a combination of the exhibitionary complex as espoused by Tony Bennett (2018) (in terms of the visitor as spectator, and as citizen to be disciplined in line with a modernist imperative) and aspects of Brian O'Doherty's (1986 [1976]) 'white cube', a pervasive (though not ubiquitous) aesthetic from the Museum of Modern Art (MoMA) onwards. These provide an historical grounding for many of the practices we still find in museums today. Andrea Witcomb (2015) adeptly synthesises these strategies in the nineteenth century museum, writing that the pedagogic quality of the museum, reinforced by 'static linear displays', positioned the visitor as citizen in opposition to the 'other' being viewed. As societal perspectives moved from singularity to plurality, the normative museum has also shifted from viewing its public as a unified citizenry to a multiplicity of audiences. However, the perceived legacies of these institutions have been difficult to shake, and the normative museum can be viewed as changing at a slower pace to that of museums established from the 1960s onwards.

In this chapter, I have chosen reference points that are generally understood as iconic on either a global level (the Tate Modern in London, the Louvre in Paris, MoMA in New York) or nationally (the National Gallery of Victoria in Australia, Staatsgalerie Stuttgart in Germany). Locating museums

DOI: 10.4324/9781003393719-4

like MoMA and the Tate Modern within the same assemblage common notion as the Louvre, Staatsgalerie Stuttgart, and the NGV might at first appear counter-intuitive. Historically, the former museums have been considered to be a break, or turning point, from the latter. What we see across the normative assemblage – within the Louvre and MoMA alike – are relations that diminish the capacity of components. This chapter illustrates the way in which control and containment strategies enter into normative component interactions. In the normative assemblage, we find a grouping of components that combine to encourage prescribed interactions for visitor movement, learning, and engagement. They also support the solidification of formal roles, including museum professionals as authorities on culture, and institutionalised processes of governance. This means that the multiplicities and potentialities of this assemblage often remain virtual, rather than actualised. The persistence of the normative as a common notion speaks to a recognisable historical trajectory, and the strength of the normative in subsuming new components into existing component relations to territorialise them.

As a common notion, the normative museum assemblage holds several 'universal singularities' that see similar practices occurring across different museums. The normative museums' priorities can be understood as holding an educative role, enlightening and civilising a 'public' as well as playing a part in nation-building. Its resources usually extend to government funding as well as comparatively stable and extensive permanent collections. Its processes include a top-down pedagogy, hierarchical management tiers, educational events, perceived highbrow publications, and prescribed movement within the museum space. The normative museums' public is catered to with a notion of 'public good' and there is the sense that visitors themselves hold a relative limited capacity to affect (in terms of movement and collaboration/feedback). Learning is predominantly relegated to a text-based communication, a privileging of vision over other senses, and the conception of museum professionals as the experts, the keepers of authoritative knowledge.

This common notion is supported by the assemblage's intersection with government policy. Through the normative museum, we see predominantly political systems intersecting with museum systems, forming a legacy of inherited policies, roles, and procedures, which consequently shape the practices that territorialise the normative museum assemblage. The expressive role includes policy documents, contractual obligations to stakeholders, and the text accompaniments to objects, which have been so routinised over time that the material roles are largely 'obedient' to the authority of the normative. As such, the normative museum is seen as the most resistant to change, because the expressive and material roles are in cohesion, thus re-territorialisation is less likely.

Today we also see corporate sponsorship and commercial activities enter into the normative assemblage. They compete with other leisure activities, provide big 'blockbuster' exhibitions, and expand their walls. The NGV is in the process of building a new building to house its contemporary works, and the Louvre has opened up internationally in Abu Dhabi. They introduce new media into exhibitions and operations, and they collaborate with communities in events and initiatives. The normative museum as a strongly held common notion subsumes these developments and components into its existing values and practices.

Normative Priorities

The priorities of the normative museum include nation-building, providing a public service role to the public (stemming from ideas around civic enlightenment and education), the conservation of the objects in the museum collection, and the development of a historical narrative. We see these clearly expressed in museum mission statements, as well as policies around acquisitions and the care of collections. These are positioned with the aim to enhance national collections and provide a public service, for the public good. Museum policies play an expressive role that interact with other components of the assemblage. For example, the Tate Britain holds specific policy documents for acquisitions (resources), care of the collections (resources), donations (resources), and ethics (processes).

References to conservation and education abound in many museum mission-statements. The care and preservation of objects feature heavily as a core premise of the museums' role in many (particularly public) art museum policies. Conservation is a priority in many museums, and it is enacted in the normative museum assemblage through a multitude of interactions that reinforce each other. In Fiona Candlin's (2010) work on the denigration of touch, the desire to avoid the contamination of and damage to objects, reaffirms a privileging of the visual over other senses. Equally, we can look to display formats like glass casing, signage, floor boundaries, security and sensors that alert security when a visitor has come to close to an artwork as contributing to both a visual spectatorship and a commitment to protecting works. Prioritising conservation often impacts on other components, with specific lighting and other display constraints (such as time between storage and the need for temperature control) affected, which in turn affects the visitor experience of the exhibition space.

A protectionist mentality can be traced through the relation between Tate's mission statement and its strategic objectives statement. The first mission set out in its governing document is 'to care for, preserve and add to the works of art and the documents in its collections.' The second and fourth statements, 'to ensure that the works of art are exhibited to the public' and to 'generally to promote the public's enjoyment and understanding of British art, and of twentieth-century and contemporary art, both by means of the Board's collections and by such other means as they consider appropriate' both position the public service role and form connections to nation-building (emphasis on 'British art') and a top-down mode of communication ('means as they consider appropriate'). The third mission is 'to ensure that the works of art and the documents are available to persons seeking to inspect them in connection with study or research' which feeds into the educative role of the normative museum. These read as predictable and traditional mission statements given the historical trajectory of normative museums. However, the Tate and MoMA go on to position these in relation to conditions of contemporaneity, giving several strategic objectives in addition to the statutory aims set out above. These are summarised as

> to consolidate, manage and research the collection in ways that respond to changes in the world around Tate; to devise innovative programmes that engage with existing and new audiences, both in the galleries and through digital media and partnerships, whose expectations of the museum are changing and whose participation will be a part of what Tate does; and to improve Tate by investing in staff development and the working culture and develop Tate's self-reliance and business model for a sustainable future.
>
> (Tate: Governance n.d.)

> Through the leadership of its Trustees and staff, The Museum of Modern Art manifests this commitment by establishing, preserving, and documenting a permanent collection of the highest order that reflects the vitality, complexity and unfolding patterns of modern and contemporary art; by presenting exhibitions and educational programs of unparalleled significance . . . Central to The Museum of Modern Art's mission is the encouragement of an ever-deeper understanding and enjoyment of modern and contemporary art by the diverse local, national, and international audiences that it serves.
>
> (MoMA: About n.d.)

We recognise the normative assemblage as 'open system', in interaction with other systems. Yet positioning these objectives within the aims of the overarching mission statement is indicative of a process that responds to exteriority by fortifying its claims to the legitimacy of its assemblage. The Tate and MoMA's mission statements show how open systems interaction are being territorialised through the expressive role.

Alongside museum mission statements, the wall placard offers another, more direct, way of communicating museum priorities to the public. There is a lot to unpick in the expressive role of wall placards, which continue to be part of the educative and disciplining aspects of normative museums. We see this in the following wall placard from Staatsgalerie Stuttgart:

> The museum is as committed to advancing research in the field of art-history as it is to reaching as wide an audience as possible. In line with its

mandate, the Staatsgalerie acquires important works of art and preserves its collection for the benefit of the public now and in the future. Take advantage of your visit today to think about the museum as an institution. The special exhibition #meinMuseum on the ground floor of the old building is a good starting point. It outlines the history of the museum in five compact time capsules.[1]

The above is a recognition of the museum's educative role (research, art-history), conservation/preservation role (acquisition and preservation of a collection) and public service role (for the benefit of the public). We see that they also hold directives for thought and movement; 'think about the museum as an institution', the ground floor as 'a good starting point'. These are subtle suggestions that nonetheless reinforce the normative common notion, by setting up a parameter for visitor engagement that encourages behaviour, movement and thought that territorialises the assemblage.

Normative Resources

At the heart of the material role in the normative museum are its collections, which intersect with the key priorities of conservation and preservation. Objects in the collection can also serve to enhance the sense of a nation-building role of the normative museum. Former Director of the Louvre (2013–2021) Jean-Luc Martinez stated in an open letter on the Louvre's website that the museum is particularly proud of the acquisition of 'national treasures'.[2] Normative museums hold permanent collections and are in the business of acquiring works by artists that are considered canonical. The canon of art history is, of course, perpetuated by these institutions in a cycle of self-legitimation. Take the Tate's Rothko Room, the Staatsgalerie's Beuys installation, the Louvre as the home of Da Vinci's *Mona Lisa* and, of course, MoMA's 'definitive' modern art collection. These all show how normative museums have developed a sense of prestige in regard to their respective collections. As such, normative museums use their collections to claim authority and legitimacy. This extends to the collections loaned for temporary blockbuster exhibitions, e.g. the NGV's yearly 'Masterpieces' exhibit. These kinds of blockbuster exhibitions reinforce authority within a network of normative museums.

There is an argument to be made for the reinforcement of a common notion through networks of art museums. In 2017, Staatsgalerie Stuttgart lent its work to five institutions, two of which were MoMA and the Tate Modern. We also saw the same process occurs between the NGV and MoMA, with the *NGV Melbourne Winter Masterpieces: MoMA 130 Years of Modern and Contemporary Art from the Museum of Modern Art, New York* (2018). A logic underpins the lending of works between institutions that hold a common notion. Artworks are components that hold a relation of exteriority – slipping in and out of different assemblage bodies. As each interaction between different bodies holds the potential to re-territorialise the assemblage, working together with other institutions that are underpinned by a similar set of practices means the likelihood of disruption is minimalised.

Normative museums have a hierarchical professional structure positioned in a way that enhances the authority of the assemblage. There is commonality in the normative museum's professional layout. Curatorial departments, conservation departments, education departments, marketing departments, and public programming departments distinguish duties within the museum. In addition, there are many external players (including technical maintenance, security, external monitoring from government bodies, laboratories, conservation professionals, and cultural contributors). Normative museums have, for the most part, perpetuated a sense of collective unity by answering to a board of trustees that operates 'in the public interest' and censoring accordingly. Manuel DeLanda states, 'Hierarchical organisations . . . depend on expressions of legitimacy, which may be embodied linguistically . . . or in the behavior of their members' (DeLanda 2006: 13). If we think about this in relation to the museum, we can follow Andrey Dewdney et al's. (2013: 186) claim that museum professionals continue to align themselves with the role of custodians in charge of object collections that have been entrenched in legitimacy, as well as 'proselytizers' for the benefits of 'communion with the museum'. Again, we see the way in which resources (in this case museum professionals and collections) play an expressive role in the assemblage. The statement by Dewdney et al. is indicative of normative relations, which reinforce professional authority and emphasise collections and collection care, as well as the art-worshipful view of 'communion with the museum'. Through this hierarchy and division of departments, we can invoke many of the same issues that Theodor Low addressed as early as 1942 during his time as a museum educator at the Metropolitan Museum New York. Citing Paul M. Rea, Low writes that there are three functions of museum activity; the acquisition and preservation of objects, the advancement of knowledge by the study of objects, and the diffusion of knowledge for the enrichment of the life of the people (Rea 1930 in Low 2012 [1942]: 36). Low goes on to write that 'the first two have forced the last to maintain a subordinate position' (Low 2012 [1942]: 36). He bemoans the way in which the 'building up of collections' and the 'scholarly prestige of the institution' have been prioritised over making the institution 'useful', claiming that museum professionals of the time feared that popularisation 'would lower standards' (Low 2012 [1942]: 37). Low saw curators, directors, and trustees as resistant to change, particularly when it came to the museum's modes of communication with the public. This contributes an explanation for why, over 80 years later, we see similar issues and themes in contemporary museum operations. Lynda Kelly writes:

> [M]useums are often locked into ways of working based on how exhibitions are developed, that is, with long timelines and (sometimes) big budgets, large project teams and not responsive to change. These processes

have resulted in a mindset of museum staff that is not attuned to working in an agile way, which relies on an iterative process and may result in releasing a product that may only be 'half-finished'.

(Kelly 2013: 62)

Unpacking this from an assemblage systems perspective, we see territorialisation in relation to temporality (long timelines) and the way in which one component (museum staff) work in reinforcing an assemblage. We see why normative practices are often reiterated in component interactions within the museum, as museum resources (staff, funding, etc.) work in reaffirming power within museum operations.

Interactions of a financial nature highlight the intersections of different assemblages to which the museum assemblage responds and reacts. A complex entanglement of assemblages is characteristic of the normative museum in terms of funding. The reality is that a publicly funded gallery is both accountable to a public and simultaneously largely underfunded, thus need substantial contributions from individual or corporate donors. Many have taken measures to territorialise financial instabilities as much as possible within their system. Judy Williams, previously the NGV's Head of Foundation reflected on the establishment of the NGV Business Council in 1988, stating that prior to this the institutions structure was focused on its public service role, rather than entrepreneurial activity (Williams in Murray 2011: 139). With the Business Council established, the NGV quickly developed its current structure, namely that it engages the business community for sponsorship. The Louvre similarly made moves to define its funding model from a position of interiority rather than a reliance on systems of exteriority, with Martinez (2014) writing that in 2009, the Louvre modernised it's financing methods through an 'endowment fund' to finance long-term projects and become more active in pursuing resources.

As a comparatively recently established museum, the Tate Modern opened in an age of economic pressure and neoliberal ideology. This integrated self-responsibility in funding from its establishment. Around and through the Tate Modern swirls a multitude of financial dealings, commercial activities, and diversified funding sources. It supplements its public funding with memberships, corporate sponsorships, commercial ventures, and entry fees for temporary exhibitions. This ecology can be seen to facilitate the entrance of new components into the museum assemblage (e.g. the introduction of marketing as a department, or reports that look at visitation success in terms of visitor numbers and financial metrics). This is a different environment to the one that saw the emergence of the Louvre, the Staatsgalerie, or the NGV, and yet across all the museums explored in this chapter there is a perceived tension or balancing act between business and culture. This is particularly evident in the controversies surrounding commercial sponsorship in the museum. Oil company BP's long-running sponsorship of the Tate and the NGV's engagement of Wilson Security to manage both NGV sites have seen large-scale backlash from citizens, artists, and activist groups. As a result, both partnerships were eventually dissolved. While this shows how component interactions can – and do – utilise their capacity to affect back on the assemblage whole, the normative museum still projects limitations on many component areas. As Derrick Chong writes, the Tate is also a brand, as much as its sponsor BP (Chong 2015: 186). In the normative museum, vested interests are spread between several bodies. Not only do you have the relationship between government, corporations, a Board of Trustees and a community, there is also the relationship between artist and other national and international museums to take into consideration. As most normative museum assemblages are to varying degrees state funded, this accountability is also evidenced in the transparency of policies and funding.

Another resource to analyse within the museum assemblage is the physical infrastructure of the museum. In this instance, I want to acknowledge the 'museum as temple' typology, but also consider expansion as a continued objective for the normative museum. For example, ever since the "Grand Louvre" project, which in 1989 doubled the available exhibition area, the Louvre has constantly sought to build, restore, or redevelop its gallery spaces to provide an optimal setting for its collections. The routinisation of mobility and expansion to territorialise a potentially destabilising force can be seen in the extension of the Louvre to Abu Dhabi. While a response to the intersection of other open systems, namely economic, cultural, and the introduction of a wider public, the Louvre projects a continuation of characteristics that further stabilise the normative assemblage. In spring of 2016, Director Martinez acted as the general curator of the opening exhibition of Louvre Abu Dhabi, an exhibition that took its focus as 'France in the Age of the Enlightenment'. We see here how the material role – in this case the systems of management and resources – contributes to the expressive role, in promoting nation-building pursuits.

The normative museum usually has either a 'single sequence' of spaces or 'variations in the singular sequence' (Tzortzi 2015: 86), creating a viewing order of objects. Museums like the Fitzwilliam in Cambridge, the Staatsgalerie in Stuttgart, and the Uffizi all hold the geography of the singular sequence. The Guggenheim Museum in New York, though organised differently in terms of spatial geography, holds the same singular sequence as a series of interconnected hallways, through its spiral arrangement. The topology of circulation, in the case of the normative assemblage, is linked to several other components performing an expressive role in addition to the material role of the architecture. With a traditional layout, art arranged on four walls around a rectangular or square room and accompanying placards, the normative museum has a linear design path and limited room for individual subversion of expectations, both in movement and in interpretation. Exhibit curator for Art/artefact (1988), Susan Vogel cites four approaches to displaying objects, two of which align with the normative assemblage. The first approach is 'anthropology exhibits' which 'explain technical, social or religious functions', the second is the 'art exhibition' in which individual objects are displayed so as to highlight their aesthetic qualities and promote a worshipful view of art (Lindauer 2006: 209). A privileging of visual experience combined with architecture, exhibition layout, social conventions, and the presence of security, invigilators, and other professional staff, tends to territorialise visitor movement as more pre-determined. This combination has been alternately referred to as 'ritual' (Duncan 1995), 'interaction order' (Goffman 1983), and 'museum discipline' (Bennett 1995; Hirschauer 2006). This kind of movement is commonly described as a slow, linear progression from one work to the next, a borderline machinic process where visitors configure themselves in a 'side by side arrangement' (Dirk vom Lehn 2013), one following the other through the exhibit. These are the instances that indicate how we arrive at the normative assemblage as a common notion. They highlight the importance of component relations between the space and visitor movement in how the visitor perceives their own capacity to affect back on the assemblage. Parts of the stabilising processes within the normative museum are formed through a (false) presentation of the museum as a closed system. In the normative museum, prescribed movement is found in the materiality of directional arrows and security/staff to point the way, in the curatorial strategies of logically ordering exhibitions rooms by artwork chronology, thematically or by artist and a lack of alternative options for negotiating desire lines built structurally into the space.

Social cues and other signifiers, like directional arrows, are likely to produce habitual movement patterns. Moving through the gallery space at Staatsgalerie Stuttgart is a chronological lesson in art history, with each numbered room devoted to a specific art movement within a certain time period. Pieces are chosen for their 'emblematic' value and positioned as canonical. There are directional arrows in each doorway, signalling the progression of art history and your prescribed route. The gallery is structured around an amphitheatre shaped sculptural garden and as it is one floor above ground, the staircase on the left facing the ticketing desk in the entry, and you descend down the right, meaning that as you systematically move through, you do not 'double back' in the gallery space. Hanging artwork is relegated to the four walls of each room, with a sculptural piece in the centre. There are normative plaques for each artwork (artist, year, medium) and headphones available for a more in-depth audio tour. The contemporary art section is thematically organised with room titles like 'land' and 'body', while the pre-enlightenment section deviates from the white walls of the other exhibition rooms, painted a deep burgundy reminiscent of the estates that would have once commissioned these pieces.

The final resource explored here is that of digital media. Every museum in this chapter has moved beyond the basic 'digital repository' of collection to operating social media accounts. Often considered a progressive shift in the museum – digital media is frequently conflated with democratic, horizontal communication models – the social media accounts of normative museums tend to indicate more continuity than change. Taking Facebook as an example, the Tate, the Louvre, Staatsgalerie Stuttgart, MoMA, and the NGV all have their comment function enabled (though editing functions are in place), allowing visitors to the site to respond to uploads from museum (media management) staff. However, the Tate and MoMA do not 'interact' with their visitors on this site, and while the Louvre occasionally 'likes' a visitor comment, this is as far as we can claim that the museum makes use of these interactive functions. Staatsgalerie Stuttgart and the NGV will occasionally 'like' a visitor comment, extending to infrequent comment 'responses' to visitor statements and questions. The Louvre and the NGV asked closed questions that fell largely into a promotional category, for example, 'Have you seen the Archaeology Goes Graphic exhibition?' (The Louvre) and 'Making plans for the school holiday?' (NGV). Staatsgalerie Stuttgart had a mixture of both open-ended and closed questions, though these were also promotional (e.g. asking 'What are you doing on vacation?' alongside a corresponding link to the current exhibition). MoMA only posted questions as a rhetorical device, answering them directly after posing them. The content across all these institutions is predominantly a combination of promotional (from current and upcoming exhibitions and event, to links to the gift shop site) and informational (primarily snapshots of artworks and artists in the collection, and some accompanying text). These findings align with Dewdney et al.'s (2013: 184) assertions around the Tate's use of digital media, which they find to be corporatist, positioning the virtual visitor as a consumer, and the interface as an opportunity to extend the Tate brand. Their study shows that through all the 'overhauls', the Tate has not strayed far from the corporatist approach to new media forms. Though surface moves towards a more open practice have been made, the depth of this is up for further analysis as agentic modes of co-production continue to be predominantly regulated. The inclusion of digital media into museums is not synonymous with democratisation of the institution and increase in visitor agency (Harrasser 2015: 383). Normative strategies around the communicative function of social media stem from minimising risk to the cultural authority of the institution, while at the same time meeting the increased expectations of engagement. What we see here is an additional system (new media) engaging with the established museum system, with the latter in many cases succeeding in territorialising the former. As a flow on effect, the visitor component is limited in exercising their expressive capacity to impact back upon the system.

Normative Publics

The normative assemblage's relationship to the public is primarily situated within priorities that express a public service and educative role, and financial activities and marketing engagement that revolve around the idea of the public as consumers. Williams has emphasised the multiple institutional narratives at the NGV, stating that they are simultaneously an education provider, a museum, an entertainment venue, a public service, and a commercial enterprise (Murray 2011: 139). The Tate's ten-year plan (spanning 2014–2024) is titled 'Championing art and its value to society'. In these examples we see three interconnected ideas that the normative museum has around its public service role. The first is the promotion of accessibility for the widest demographic possible. The second, that the museum positions art as an asset for 'promoting encounters', thus 'championing art'. Finally, from 'a forum', to 'dialogue', to 'value to society', the normative museum strives to position its relationship to the public as 'democratic'. Historical significance plays an important role here. Public accessibility follows one of the main threads of museum history from the early establishment of public museums. The newer emphasis on hospitality (openness and responsiveness) aims to combat the criticisms directed at art museums (for being exclusionary and authoritarian).

Museums are increasingly engaged in public outreach. In June of 2014, the Louvre developed an agreement with the Prisons Administration Department, forming a new partnership with the École Nationale de l'Administration Pénitentiaire (National School of Penitentiary Administration). However, these kinds of outreach programmes affirm a Foucauldian governmental perspective, which sees the museums role as civilising. The normative museums' role is pedagogical and aims to educate a citizenry on the national imaginary and corresponding national ideals, promote ideas of modernity and progression and to build communities by treating visitors as a unified whole, as opposed to individually.

While we see 'democratising' practices and community engagement as desired objectives within museum practice today, in the normative museum assemblage, engagement with the public territorialise ideas around expertise and hierarchies of knowledge. In communicating with the public, the normative museum assemblage encourages a singular authoritative voice. Even museums that have been touted as 'cutting-edge', or that attempt to introduce a multiplicity of perspectives, do so in a way that maintains institutional hierarchy. Pedro Lorente (2015: 124–125) points to this through the Tate Modern's *The Bigger Picture* exhibition, which provided dual wall texts – one written by an anonymous museum staff member, the 'supplementary text' written by a celebrity. By keeping the institutional labels anonymous, they are positioned as objective truth, rather than personal opinion, thus limiting the plurality of discourses.

Ien Ang's (2015) study of the Art Gallery of New South Wales' 2001–2002 exhibition Buddha: Radiant Awakening found that the historical legacy of art legitimisation and authority runs deep in museums and creates boundaries for what is considered acceptable in terms of community involvement and engagement. Ang writes about professional staff – namely curatorial – overruling community suggestions on the grounds of community lacking the necessary expertise. This aligns with the resource component expressed earlier, and indicates that there are distinct, unwritten terms, which delimit community involvement in exhibition making. We can see this delineation occurring in consistent, yet subtle ways across numerous components with which the museum visitor interacts. In Staatsgalerie Stuttgart, for example:

> The anniversary exhibition #meinMuseum ['my museum'] offers visitors a wide range of opportunities to join in. For example, you can 'like' your favourite Staatsgalerie painting. If you go to the Digital Collection section of our website, you can explore the collection and pic out your personal favourites by clicking on the little heart symbol to the right of the image.[3]

During the run of the #meinMuseum exhibition (2018) at Staatsgalerie Stuttgart, the works voted as favourites were put on temporary display, on a wall proclaiming in large signage '#meinMuseum Ihr Lieblingsstück der Woche' (#myMuseum, Your favourite piece of the week). This is indicative of the way in which museums are aiming to democratise the museum through digital media engagement. It is a way of increasing the visitor component's capacity to affect (moving towards a feedback loop characteristic of emergent assemblages). And yet, when we consider the relations between the different components involved in the #meinMuseum activity, we see some processes emerging that are consistent with the normative assemblage. For example, the visitor is only able to 'like' their favourite work by clicking on the little heart symbol. This gives the museum an idea about which works are the most liked, but it does not offer the opportunity for visitors to explain why they like what they like. If the latter were an option, visitors would have a chance at contributing a narrative about the artworks that could parallel, augment, or disrupt the art historical narrative projected by Staatsgalerie Stuttgart. In turn, they would be afforded an enhanced capacity to affect back on the assemblage.

Nearly all museums have terms and conditions for public entry. In the normative museum, no-touch is privileged as the default (Classen 2005; Dudley 2010). The NGV Terms and Conditions states, 'Whenever you are on NGV Premises you need to refrain from: touching, or in any other way, interfering with artwork on display' (NGV: Terms and Conditions n.d.). Another commonly held rule is around sound. On the Louvre website (Louvre: Museum Rules n.d.), under the auspices of 'respecting artworks', visitors are explicitly told to refrain from making too much noise. Within the Tate Britain's 'Policies and Procedures' document is a subsection titled 'Tate Gallery Rules', which includes the statement 'Please respect the rights of other visitors to quiet contemplation and study' (Tate: Policies and Procedures, n.d.). This reveals an entrenched notion that art is there to be both revered and to play an educative role. The normative museum promotes an art-worshipful view of the objects housed within its walls, and we see this reiterated both in the process of curatorial strategies and the positioning of visitors as spectators.

Normative Processes

'Processes' illustrates how the capacities of expressive and material roles are enacted in the museum space. Even though a rhetoric of accessibility and inclusivity abounds in the normative museum, the way in which this assemblage communicates to the public is through educational events and highbrow publications. This kind of top-down educational strategy leads to a particular demographic (tertiary educated, higher income earners) frequenting the museum, while other demographics remain alienated. More often than not, normative museum visitors are familiar with the social etiquettes and rules of the normative museum (follow the signage, if you must talk, make it a low murmur, don't touch the artwork). In turn, little occurs in the way of deterritorialisation and the visitor reinforces the normative common notion as they interact with other components.

The normative museum tends to be caught in a negotiation between private stakeholders, government policy and the public it serves, particularly in an age where they must legitimate themselves both culturally and financially. In light of this, their operations are often limited and less experimental. As Richard Sandell states:

> We have traditionally been very risk-averse and very conservative in museums and we tend to view conflict and controversy as something we'd like to avoid. It's something which is viewed as a sign perhaps of failure and not of success.
>
> (2016: 593)

What we have seen as a continuous thread across the practices of the normative museum is a 'control and containment' strategy, from how artwork is displayed, signage about 'proper' visitor behaviour in the space, the way in which digital media engagement is limited, to strictly enforced professional hierarchies that see decisions going through a lengthy approval chain.

Normative museums reference the objective of progression and responsiveness to contemporary conditions. At face value, the acknowledgement of this as a priority would indicate an openness to dynamism and change. When we look to how these priorities are enacted through the interactions between resources and publics (digital media operations are a particularly pertinent example), the sense that normative museums are receptive to change is lessened. Insights into the components of priorities, resources, processes and publics, which together form the common notion of the normative museum (and simultaneously problematise the 'typology' of a 'traditional' museum), show how component interactions work together in order to reinforce the assemblage. While the normative museum is no less exposed to the conditions of mobility and reflexivity than any other museum assemblage, what is notable about normative museum practice is the way in which it is systematically territorialised. The legitimisation of the authority of the normative museum type is evident in the obedience of these components with one another. This is not to say that the normative museum has not faced tensions within components of the assemblage. Rather, the power of an entrenched expressive role – ritualised through the resources, processes and publics – territorialises the influences of other open systems of assemblage. This results in the continuation of practices that inform the curatorial strategies and visitor experience of normative museums.

In the following chapters, I evaluate how components exercise a different set of capacities through their interactions to produce responsive, affective, and emergent common notions. Conversely, I also provide examples where museums have taken on qualities of the normative assemblage in order to re-territorialise from responsive, affective, and emergent to a normative common notion.

Notes

1 Transcribed from wall placard, visitation July 2018.
2 This statement takes on an unsavoury taste given that in May of 2022, Martinez was charged in connection with alleged antiquities trafficking.
3 Transcribed from wall placard, visitation July 2018.

References

#meinMuseum. (2018). Staatsgalerie Stuttgart, Stuttgart. Exhibition viewed June 30, 2018.

Ang, Ien (2015). 'Change and Continuity: Art Museums and the Reproduction of Art Museumness'. A. Witcomb and K. Message (eds.) *The International Handbooks of Museum Studies: Museum Theory*. Cambridge, MA/Oxford: Wiley Blackwell. Pp. 211–232.

Bennett, Tony (1995). *The Birth of the Museum: History, Theory, Politics*. London: Routledge.

Bennett, Tony (2018). *Museums, Power, Knowledge: Selected Essays*. Oxon/New York: Routledge.

Candlin, Fiona (2010). *Art, Museums and Touch*. Manchester: Manchester University Press.

Chong, Derrick (2015). 'Tate and BP – Oil and Gas as the New Tobacco? Arts Sponsorship, Branding, and Marketing'. Conal McCarthy (ed.) *The International Handbooks of Museum Studies: Museum Practice*. Malden/Oxford: Wiley Blackwell. Pp. 179–202.

Classen, Constance (2005). *The Book of Touch*. Oxford: Berg.

DeLanda, Manuel (2006). *A New Philosophy of Society: Assemblage Theory and Social Complexity*. London/New York: Continuum.

Dewdney, Andrew, David Dibosa and Victoria Walsh (2013). *Post Critical Museology: Theory and Practice in the Art Museum*. London: Routledge.

Dudley, Sandra (2010). *Museum Materialities: Objects, Engagements, Interpretations.* Oxon & New York: Routledge.

Duncan, Carol (1995). *Civilising Rituals: Inside Public Art Museums.* London & New York: Routledge.

Goffman, Erving (1983). 'The Interaction Order: American Sociological Association, 1982 Presidential Address'. *American Sociological Review* 48(1). Pp. 1–17.

Harrasser, Karin (2015). '(Dis)playing the Museum: Artifacts, Visitors, Embodiment, and Mediality'. M. Henning (ed.) *International Handbook of Museum Studies: Museum Media.* Malden/Oxford: Wiley Blackwell. Pp. 371–388.

Hirschauer, Stefan (2006). 'Animated Corpses: Communicating with Post Mortals in an Anatomical Exhibition'. *Body & Society* 12(4). Pp. 25–52.

Kelly, Lynda (2013). 'The Connected Museum in the World of Social Media'. K. Drotner and K. Schroder (eds.) *Museum Communication and Social Media: The Connected Museum.* London: Routledge. Pp. 54–71.

Lindauer, M. (2006). 'The Critical Museum Visitor'. J. Marstine (ed.) *New Museum Theory and Practice: An Introduction.* Malden/Oxford/Victoria: Blackwell. Pp. 201–225.

Lorente, Pedro (2015). 'From White Cube to a Critical Museography: The Development of Interrogative, Plural and Subjective Museum Discourses'. Katarzyna Murawska Muthesius and Piotr Priotrowski (eds.) *From Museum Critique to the Critical Museum.* Surrey/Burlington: Ashgate. Pp. 115–128.

Louvre: Museum Rules (n.d.). https://www.louvre.fr/en/visit/museum-rules, last accessed 28 January 2023.

Low, Theodore (2012 [1942]). 'What is a Museum'? G. Anderson (ed.) *Reinventing the Museum: The Evolving Conversation on the Paradigm Shift* (2nd ed.). Plymouth: AltaMira Press.

Martinez, Jean-Luc (2014). 'Director's Message'. https://www.louvre.fr/en/missions-projects, last accessed 30 March 2014.

MoMA: About (n.d.). https://www.moma.org/about/who-we-are/moma, last accessed 16 December 2015.

Murray, Phip (2011). *The NGV Story; A Celebration of 150 Years.* Melbourne: National Gallery of Victoria.

NGV. (2018). *Melbourne Winter Masterpieces: MoMA, 130 Years of Modern and Contemporary Art from the Museum of Modern Art, New York.* National Gallery of Victoria, Melbourne. Exhibition. Viewed August 20, 2018.

NGV: Terms and Conditions (n.d.). https://www.ngv.vic.gov.au/about/reports-anddocuments/terms-and-conditions-of-public-entry/, last accessed 20 December 2017.

O'Doherty, Brian (1986 [1976]). *Inside the White Cube: The Ideology of the Gallery Space.* San Francisco: The Lapis Press.

Sandell, Richard (2016). 'A Reflection on Participation'. Kayte McSweeney and Jen Kavanagh (eds.) *Museum Participation: New Directions for Audience Collaboration.* Edinburgh, UK: MuseumsEtc. Pp. 578–601.

Tate: Governance (n.d.). https://www.tate.org.uk/governance, last accessed 14 June 2016.

Tate: Policies and Procedures (n.d.). https://www.tate.org.uk/visit/tate-gallery-rules, last accessed 28 January 2023.

Tzortzi, Kali (2015). *Museum Space: Where Architecture Meets Museology.* London/ New York: Routledge.

Vogel, Susan. (1988). *ART/ artifact*. Center for African Art, New York City. Exhibition.

Vom Lehn, Dirk (2013). 'Withdrawing from Exhibits: The Interactional Organisation of Museum Visits'. Pentti Haddington, Lorenza Mondada and Maurice Nevile (eds.) *Interaction and Mobility: Language and the Body in Motion*. Berlin: De Gruyter. Pp. 65–90.

Witcomb, Andrea (2015). 'Cultural Pedagogies in the Museum'. M. Watkins, G. Noble and C. Driscoll (eds.) *Cultural Pedagogies and Human Conduct*. London/New York: Routledge.

4 The Responsive Museum
Community and Constituents

Almost two decades ago, Caroline Lang et al. (2006) explored the term 'responsive museum' and its associated practices. They primarily align features of responsiveness with audience services (accessibility, learning-focused, targeting programming, etc.), though they also include 'promoting professionalism', seen as encouraging and supporting staff to learn, experiment and reflect (Lang et al. 2006: 227–228). One function of the responsive museum is to enhance community control of the museum, and be in dialogue with audiences, moving beyond consulting into 'seriously listening' (Lang et al. 2006: 227). Their definition of the responsive museum invokes a duality between museum visitors being viewed as a 'consumer', or/and as a 'learner'. Alongside the former lays connotations of the museums role as being part of the 'entertainment/service' industry, the latter as an educative institute.

This chapter takes the term 'responsive museum' along a different trajectory. Rather than aligning with the tradition of visitor studies that has developed in response to marketing, enterprise, and audience demand/consumption, I see a responsive common notion as developing practices that privilege the idea of museum communities. As the museum assemblage intersected with other social assemblages – namely post-colonial and feminist assemblages – a shift towards more community-oriented and collaborative processes occurred. Andrea Witcomb (2015: 160) writes that while the pedagogical strategy of the nineteenth century can still be seen in some exhibitions today, the identity politics and social movements of the 1960s and 1970s did serve to change museum practice. Witcomb's assertion indicates that in addition to the normative assemblage, another common notion developed. We can contextualise the responsive common notion through what Gerald Raunig (2009) refers to as the first and second phases of institutional critique.[1]

The first phase of institutional critique can be summarised by three core interlocking themes, all of which continue to be critically explored today. First, the way in which art had been framed by enlightenment rationality no longer served to encapsulate the complexity of artworks and art practice. Second, the role the museum played in defining the value of art, particularly in an ever-burgeoning art market, required critical consideration. Third, the

DOI: 10.4324/9781003393719-5

exclusionary practices of museums were detrimental to artists, publics, and the museum itself. This manifested in two ways: the inclusion of identity politics in debates around museum representation and the development of new 'alternative' spaces for the exhibition of art. What is key to understanding the first wave of institutional critique is that these criticisms and the practices associated with them have gradually been subsumed by the institution.

The second phase, most prominent in the late 1980s into the 1990s (Raunig 2009: 3), is categorised by institutional critique from within.[2] By 'within', we can understand this phase as operating from the standpoint of artists having 'inevitable involvement in the institution' (Raunig 2009: 9), and museums as unable to operate oblivious to institutional critique. Concurrently, scholarship became a growing field not only in museum education and conservation but also in identity politics and representation. Academic works debating the political nature of museums called for a more engaged approach to communities and the introduction of diversity into the museums, as well as a rethinking of assumptions around their authority to tell stories and assert ownership of collections. This further propelled a constructive push towards dialogue between museums and the communities whose cultures and traditions were represented therein. We began to see questions of democratising practice move to the forefront of museum critique, through discussion around issues of inclusion, access, and comfortability for marginalised and formerly colonised people entering into museum spaces.

In 1989, Peter Vergo coined the term 'new museology' to describe this more critically aware phase in the approach to museum studies. New museology is seen to sit in opposition to the 'adoring art historical model' whereby museums and museologists position art as 'sacred', separate to everyday life, and 'a source of moral authority' (Pollock 2007: 1). Instead, new museology aims to avoid the trap of overgeneralisation and parallels the transformation of the museum from a site of worship and awe to one of discourse and critical reflection. As a result, it looks at how museums not only represent cultural identity but also produce it through framing, declaring itself an 'active player in the making of meaning' (Marstine 2006: 4–5). This aligns with Raunig's claim that the second phase of institutional critique can be generally defined as self-reflexive operation from within the institution.

A more recent extension of the critique of museums in terms of representation and collaboration can be linked to the concept of 'slow museology', developed by Raymond Silverman. As a concept, it serves as a practical application of collaboration between community and museum, which negotiates the 'incompatibilities of "collaborative time" and "institutional time"' (Silverman 2015: 13). This focuses on the challenges of reconnecting museums with their local communities, offering 'slow museology' as a necessary component when approaching such a project. This came as a response to a perceived 'failure' of collaboration between museum professionals and a community, which were largely due to the discrepancies between museum deadlines for exhibition and the lengthy processes of forming a nuanced (re) presentation of both tangible and intangible cultural heritage.[3] Silverman argues that these failures are in fact successes, as they open space for new sensitivities and present unconsidered questions (2015: 2). This mirrors Ivan Karp and Corinne Kratz's (2015) writing on the 'interrogative museum', who write that in the interrogative framework, collaborative projects establish a pluralism that accounts for both museum and community knowledges. As a consequence, this subtly challenges and reshapes museum authority (Karp and Kratz 2015: 294). Similarly, Witcomb's call for a 'pedagogy of listening', which is 'as much a metaphor here as an embodied actual practice' (2015: 160), includes representing a multiplicity of voices within the museum, as well as incorporating interactives that afforded the visitor the capacity of an 'active learner'. These practices are integral to our understanding of the responsive museum assemblage, which sees a reframing of museum–public relations with the initial aim of redressing the exclusion and marginalisation of women and people of colour in the museum. Later this came to be extended to thinking more about how museums could better engage people living with disability (Sandell 2016, 2019). Across these wider societal progressions are questions of access, representation, and presence.

The responsive museum epitomises the idea of social movements as a hybrid of interpersonal networks and institutional organisations. These are seen to give rise to organisations to stabilise social movements and perform specialised functions. As such, the use of the term 'responsive' in this work supports the analysis done by John Byrne and his collaborators around 'constituent' museums. They write:

> As museums begin to see themselves as sites of collaborative knowledge production, and begin to replay their earlier, nineteenth-century roles as active sites for the co-production of new civic identities, it became apparent that the terms use and usership did not fully implicate the necessity for museums to re-think their own operating systems and managerial structures. Or, to put this another way, it began to seem apparent that museums could do little more than 're-brand' their existing relationships with audiences– as the one-way and non-reciprocal broadcast of established knowledge– unless museums were prepared to open themselves up to the reciprocal possibility of change.
>
> (Byrne et al. 2018: 11)

Resistance to Change: Distinguishing Normative and Responsive Practice

While claims of increased access and representation now abound in museum mission statements, this does not always extend to collaborative practices. 'Opening up' and 'reciprocity' have not been uniformly adopted, and the normative assemblage's claims to legitimacy and authority (see Chapter 3) often suppress the possibility of change. And so, while there has been a widespread assertion of typically 'responsive' characteristics in museums, these do not necessarily constitute a responsive assemblage. Ien Ang's case study of the Art Gallery of New South Wales (AGNSW) exemplifies this discrepancy. The case study revolved around the temporary exhibition *Buddha: Radiant Awakening* (2001–2002). Early into the exhibition, community focus groups signalled interest in a broader cultural focus of Buddhism, rather than 'just art'. The public engagement and audience development activities surrounding the exhibition signified a 'disjuncture of "culture" (in the broad anthropological sense) and "art" (in the specialised aesthetic sense)' (Ang 2015: 219). In response, AGNSW widened the exhibition to include a 'Wisdom Room' for public expression, such as 'tea ceremonies, mandala making, chanting, and meditation sessions' (Ang 2015: 219). Here we see an initial play towards responsiveness by the museum. However, Ang notes that while the Wisdom Room was popular among audiences and saw a strong level of participation, it was ultimately a 'peripheral add-on' that did not challenge the gallery's claim to specialist knowledge (2015: 219). Consequently, responsiveness does not become embedded in museum component relations and the museum is not re-territorialised as a responsive common notion.

The example of *Buddha: Radiant Awakening* showcases a particular resistance to change. What was witnessed by the researchers of this project was a point at which the art museum and its professionals claimed their own authority and self-legitimised. In a 2001 interview with Ang, Jackie Menzies (head curator of Asian art at AGNSW) intimated that, although the AGNSW had the desire to involve people, ultimately specialist knowledge (coming from the institution) trumped community involvement (Ang 2015: 219). Attempts at opening up the museum to community involvement can be seen as an 'assimilatory project', whereby the new visitor is ideally initiated into the art world, reinforcing an aesthetic disposition and sense of curatorial control. Even if intentions are good, the institution is held back by its historical legacy (Ang 2015: 216). Intimated here is the difficulty of re-territorialising normative assemblage relations, which have a long temporal span as a common notion.

Indications that museums are retaining their normative practice, rather than affording responsive component interactions, are echoed elsewhere. Elizabeth Crooke references a UK study (Lynch 2011) on museums and their communities, which found that despite more avenues for inclusion, community partners were often relegated to the role of 'supplicant', rather than 'active agent' (Crooke 2015: 481). These kinds of relations between professionals and community suggest that while museums see the social benefit of inclusion and participation, museum professionals tend to place more value on traditional forms of 'expertise'.

The perceived boundary between museum/art expert and the contributions of community members are an element of museum practice that intersect between the normative and the responsive museum. Because of the overlaps between the normative and responsive museum in terms of their priorities (namely 'to educate'), a deeper look at the ways in which those priorities are mobilised through practice is necessary to distinguish the two. The crucial distinction here is that, in responsive museums, collaborative qualities allow for feedback from the public(s), but no feedback loop. That is to say, the capacity for the community to exercise a role remains limited in the responsive museum assemblage. Nonetheless, the normative and the responsive are distinguishable because the latter has shifted from the *representation* of communities, to the *presence* of communities within museum practice.

This chapter takes two museums as its point of focus in exploring responsive museum practice. The first is Te Papa in Wellington, Aotearoa/New Zealand. The second is Moderna Galerija (MG) in Ljubljana, Slovenia. The former has a specific relationship with community, one that is supported by Aotearoa/New Zealand's governmental status as bicultural. The latter likewise holds a strong community focus. However, MG inverses the relationship with government, seeing itself as picking up public responsibilities when governments are restricted. Both see meaning in the museum as a co-produced process, working towards enhancing a public sense of ownership through inclusive and democratising practices. In the final part of this chapter, the work of Paul Tapsell (2015) on the historical trajectory of Auckland Museum (Aotearoa/New Zealand) highlights the slow process of re-territorialisation from a normative common notion (see Chapter 3) to a responsive practice.

Responsive Priorities

The responsive museum's priorities are typical of what Tony Bennett calls 'simultaneously epistemological and civic' (2013: 53). The focus on education and conservation found in the mission statements of normative museums is carried over into the responsive museum. In the case of Te Papa, they are extended to include a focus on cultural heritage and address multiple publics. Like the normative museum, Te Papa is at an intersection with governmental policies, although with an 'arms-length' model of governance that gives the museum more authority in responding to community needs. In the 'arms-length' model, the government both funds and owns cultural institutions, and appoints their governing boards. While they must regard central government policies from the New Zealand Ministry for Culture and Heritage (NZ MCH), government funded museums in Aotearoa/New Zealand hold the agency to implement their own policies, ideally developing a cultural industry without undue government interference. Te Papa has 'policy and practice developed specifically in response to the demand by *iwi*[4] that they be consulted on the care, interpretation and display of their culture' (McCarthy 2019: 38). The operations and networks in place at the museum emphasise the repatriation and care of heritage items with their source communities involved in this process (Te Papa Annual Report 2017–2018: 9).

There is a heightened sense of locality within the responsive assemblage, which emerges through a variety of different interactions between priorities, resources, and publics. This is evident at both MG and Te Papa through a focus on collecting artwork by Slovenian artists in the former, and Aotearoa/ New Zealand artists in the latter. MG's vision statement contains numerous references to locality, for example:

> Moderna galerija attempts to develop a different model of museum based on the criticism and redefinition of democratic institution. Its priorities include the construction of a local context and dialogues with different localities that follow especially similar priorities and interests in developing different institutionality and new models of cultural production.
> (MG & MSUM Website: Vision Statement n.d.)

As we see in the above statement, this community focus translates into the way in which responsive museums develop networks. For MG, its two largest collaborative networks, *L'Internationale* and *New Mappings of Europe* are both framed in terms of a local–global connection. For *L'Internationale*, MG writes:

> L'Internationale proposes a space for art within a non-hierarchical and decentralised internationalism, based on the values of difference and horizontal exchange among a constellation of cultural agents, locally rooted and globally connected.

For New Mappings of Europe, MG states that the core purpose of this project is to 'generate knowledge about the migrants' cultural heritage in Europe and make cultural and art institutions more accessible to local communities of migrants of the first and second generations as well as to the new communities of asylum seekers and refugees' (MG & MSUM Website: Collaborations n.d.).

At Te Papa, we can see this connection to locality and network through their strategic priorities. The document outlining the strategic priorities for 2017–2021 at Te Papa contained several aims that are common to most museums – business growth, exhibition renewal, digital experience, and fostering 'core business' (in the case of Te Papa this is the care and preservation of national collections; fostering learning programmes and research; and providing support for museums, galleries, and *iwi* across Aotearoa/New Zealand). However, the strategic priorities also take on a more localised and community focus, extending to *iwi* engagement, taking a lead in important national conversations, and the creation of a learning hub in Auckland (Te Papa Annual Report 2017–2018: 12).

Responsive Museum Resources

Two other core priorities expressed within responsive museum documents are accountability to the public and accessibility. As expressive roles within mission statements, these objectives play a material role when it comes to resources. An example of this process can be seen in Richard Sandell's research into disability access within museums. The responsive museum is positioned as publicly 'accessible' (Lang et al. 2006), for example, its cost barrier is kept low, and the language it uses in marketing and wall labels are less 'cerebral' and more 'readable'. Another level of access important to the responsive museum is physical access. In many museums, physical access to the museum falls under resources, as it is linked to the relations between building layout, exhibition design, and those with mobility aids or hearing and visual impairments. In the responsive museum, the process of accessibility is extended. We see through the following example that when we talk about 'access' as a resource in museums, the mobilisation of further participatory relations is the process by which the responsive assemblage is recognised. In a 2016 interview, Sandell talks about the relationship set up between the Draw-bridge Group (a disability consultative group) and the Nottingham Museums in the 1990s during his time working there. He acknowledges that it was not until the consultants – recruited to help increase accessibility in the museum – articulated the lack of disability-representation within museum spaces, that the museum began to take stock of its practices of inclusivity and make changes accordingly (Sandell in McSweeney and Kavanagh 2016: 588). That work continues today, with Sandell claiming that after 2010, museums have become far more politically engaged around the topic of visibility and representation. This sustained engagement indicates a prolonged temporal scale towards the responsive. In the example above, Drawbridge Group represents another component slotting into the museum assemblage. They then went on to exercise an expressive role – questioning the limitations placed on their capacity to affect – which in turn shaped the assemblage whole. The component of 'established' museum professionals then developed the boundaries for how this politics of representation would enter the museum.

It is at the intersection of funding and professional staff, that MG makes a remarkable case for the responsive assemblage. Curator Tjaša Pogačar Podgornik, writing on the MG exhibition/project *Every Man is a Curator* (2007), provides insight into the intersection of state and museum. Pogačar Podgornik (2018: 276–277) references strategies of artists' self-organisation as a reactive countermeasure to 'the degradation of state support structures' and the 'entrepreneurialization of culture'. This strategy necessitates the opening up of institutions to public participation and non-institutional actors to gain traction in the museum space, which MG is seen as having accomplished in this instance. While I made the case in priorities around the link between governmental policy and the responsive assemblage for Te Papa, we see a different kind of government–museum relationship arises in MG, though it is no less responsive for it. In fact, Pogačar Podgornik sees this relationship as 'a form of support to and solidarity with an institution in crisis' (2018: 277). This indicates a broader kind of responsiveness. Bearing witness to the diminishing power of the state in the face of neoliberalism, MG has considered how institutions remain not only relevant but places with an enduring role as a public service. Taking this stance prioritises the notion of public as citizens over public as consumers, linking back to Byrne et al.'s (2018) premise for the 'constituent museum'.

The inclusion of Māori in the daily operations of the museum, alongside the understanding objects as *taonga* and museums as guardians, rather than owners of *taonga*, makes headway in 'transforming the house'. The inclusion of components like the *Waharoa* (welcoming gateway) in the grand foyer of Te Papa, and signage in both English and te reo Māori, position the visitor experience of the museum in relation to Māori culture from entry. This is crucial, as the single authorial voice of normative museums is difficult to re-territorialise in spaces where this expressive role is physically embedded. In the case of MG, re-territorialisation occurs through alternate forms of self-organisation, with the help of its networks of constituents.

If the normative museum positioned individual memory as subjective, unreliable, and strictly separate to an authorised official history, the responsive museum challenges this. Individual memory becomes not only acceptable for inclusion but a key tool in transmitting a historical narrative. In the responsive museum, video becomes a key medium in this transmission. Steffi de Jong (2015) argues that the specific aesthetic of video testimonies, particularly their conversational framing, actually reinforces long-established priorities of the museum. While the affective potential of video remains, the documentary aesthetic favoured in responsive museum displays adheres to the transmission of historical information and moral message found in traditional museums.

At Te Papa's physical site, various interactives afford different levels of interactions. Digital interactives are utilised in a more nuanced way through the ethnographic collections, than they are through the art collections. For example, in the Te Māori exhibit, several screens are positioned alongside each other in the centre of a dimly lit room, each with another screen backing them so one must walk the circumference in order to view them all. Each presents a video testimonial of an immigrant story. Instead of having headphones to listen to each interview individually, one must enter into close proximity with each screen in turn, in order to separate each speaker from their neighbours.

In Te Papa, video testimonials are used in the same conversational way posited by de Jong (2015). However, I found that rather than a normative transmission of historical information, the testimonials at Te Papa provided several counterhistories, with each of the several screens devoted to an immigrant story. The 'moral message' comes from the curatorial strategies in framing this interaction, rather than the recorded content. These particular video testimonies of immigrant stories at Te Papa require an active listening on behalf of the visitor. Because of the proximity of the screens to each other, one has to step closer to a screen. This puts the visitor literally face to face with speaker, creating an intimacy in the interaction. The sound level of the interview recording means that in order to clearly hear their individual testimony this proximity is necessary. This isn't a traditional object–subject relationship within the museum, this is a subject–subject relationship, and each story must be taken individually. The 'moral message' is an embodied one, experienced by the visitor through their engagement with the video testimonials.

Digital interactives in the art collections of Te Papa are markedly different. In one room, a touch screen is built into a table, with room for two people to sit at a time. From the screen, one is able to select a painting from the wall directly opposite, with a zoom function to look at the work in detail. Information about artistic process is accompanied by infrared images of the work if one holds one's fingertip on the image on screen. The use of digital interactives in the art collection of Te Papa are indicative of a kind of technological interactivity that maintains a traditional, authoritative museum narrative. This interactive largely serves the purpose of communicating the priority of conservation, shaping the experience as a predominantly normative interaction through the authorial voice of a museum professional.

Responsive Museum Publics

The responsive museum is more inclined to view their visitors as constituents. Further, it takes a mixture of component alignment and component conflict to create a genuine shift from community representation to community presence within the museum. In Te Papa, we have already explored this through the professional staff component, and the way in which they work together with *iwi* in order to prioritise the Māori relationship to *taonga*. However, this is not the only constituency of Te Papa to be included within the museum. One does not have to dig deep to find other points of intersection whereby constituents are afforded a greater capacity to affect back on the assemblage. For example:

> Collaborative work with students from Wellington High School in support of Toi Art provided new opportunities for students to gain deeper access to collections and explore complex issues. Students were initially invited to act as an advisory group but their engagement provided a source of rich input informing exhibition design, audience interactions and public programming opportunities.
>
> (Te Papa Annual Report 2017–2018: 25)

The key here is in the distinction between 'advisory group' and 'a source of rich input' informing various aspects of museum practice. In a responsive assemblage, we see interactions occur that afford the communities/constituents interacting with the assemblage a greater capacity to affect back on the assemblage whole. As we see, this impacts on numerous other component relations – 'exhibition design, audience interactions and public programming'. We see a similar story in the practices of MG, through the intersection of refugee and migrant communities. Senior curator for education and public programmes at MG, Adela Železnik (2018: 58–59) reflects on the relationships MG built with former residents of Bosnia-Herzegovina in the 1990s, and connects this with the 2017 development of an alternative cultural association run by recent migrants to Slovenia, as well as a series of embroidery workshops held for female asylum seekers from Iran and Afghanistan. For the latter, this brought together local women, the recent migrants, as well as the original migrants from Bosnia-Herzegovina. As we see, the responsive territorialisation of MG has a long history.[5] Having already realised their relationship to migrant communities from the 1990s, MG has territorialised habits in place to continue to be responsive to changing constituencies. As new constituents (migrants and refugees) come to intersect with the art institution, they find that space has already been carved out for them. We see through the inclusion of work opportunities (extending to management), as well as the collaborative workshops facilitated by the museum, that the interaction aligns more with presence than representation.

These examples indicate that in the responsive assemblage, the museum develops relationships with a variety of publics. As an extension of this, we see many instances of responsive assemblages happening art museum-adjacent places. This highlights what I have previously posited, which is that the responsive museum assemblage relies on intersections with other established assemblages, often various community or government bodies. As an example, we can turn to Bojana Piškur's project study of *Radical Education* (RE) at MG. RE began in 2006, with the occupation of a bicycle factory in Ljubljana and centred around a series of seminars, debates, exhibitions, and researches in the intersection between the 'museum' and the 'movement' (Piškur 2018: 175). The 'movement' in this instance was a politics of the now, expressed through the inclusion of social centres, artistic and political collectives, and local community into discussions with the museum. A core aim was to 'define common investigations between the two fields, i.e. art and politics' (Piškur 2018: 176). According to Piškur (2018: 175):

> In RE, from the very beginning, the ways of opening up the museum for various 'publics' were deliberated, bringing different practices from the 'outside' into the very context of an art institution as well as creating common micro-political situations through different alliances and collective actions. However, at the same time RE was also a rather heterogenous group of people with different backgrounds and experiences of working

in communities and institutions, so as a consequence, very different and sometimes rather conflictual ideas arose on what kind of space a museum actually was.

There are several points to highlight in this statement with relation to the responsive assemblage. First, the idea of 'opening up' the museum to include multiple public(s) voices, a feature of the responsive assemblage already articulated. Second, the idea of 'deliberation', which implies a process aligned with Raymond Silverman's (2015) ideas around slow museology.[6] Third, the idea of 'alliances and collective actions' in conjunction with 'conflictual ideas'. An assemblage comes into itself as a common notion when components work in alliance to create the sense that a variety of different components interact to form a 'body' that can be perceived as a (bounded) whole. However, this is a constant process of negotiation, one that experiences 'conflictual ideas' if components do not exercise their material or expressive role in a way that aligns with the assemblage whole. RE is made up of a variety of destabilising components – an accurate reflection of the public as constituents – who, though at times conflicting, assert themselves in a collective way to form an assemblage that in turn is destabilising for MG. This final point is particularly important when we consider how this relationship between RE and MG played out. Piškur (2018: 177) writes:

> In 2014 RE came to the point where this kind of intervention in the space of an art institution became unnecessary. Certainly, not unnecessary in the sense that the museum became an ideal institution, but that the ideas of RE in a way had become embedded in debates on 'other institutionality' within the museum itself.

We can interpret this activity, and the consequent 'embeddedness' of RE into MG, as a social assemblage intersecting with an institutional assemblage and the former territorialising the latter as a responsive assemblage.

Responsive Museum Processes

In the responsive museum, priorities, resources, and publics work together to create moments of interaction that allow for marginalised voices to be heard and multiple perspectives to emerge. We see, through the processes that make up the practices to qualify a responsive museum assemblage, that the public(s) surrounding the museum are afforded a greater affective capacity. Yet we also can observe that the institution carefully manages this capacity, with measures taken to minimise risk to museum legitimacy and authority. We see the breadth of this process in a case study by Professor Paul Tapsell from his time as Tumuaki (Director Māori) at Auckland Museum.

Nowadays, Aotearoa/New Zealand is renowned for its institutional collaboration with Māori communities. But, as Tapsell indicates, this wasn't always the case. He writes 'Since 1852 the relationship between Auckland Museum and its 800 plus source-*marae*[7] communities has generally been one-way, with curators only engaging our communities when they sought objects or information' (Tapsell 2015: 270). There are several points through which this is seen to have shifted into an institutional framework that is more inclusive and community oriented. These are situated as moments of historical significance, the principles of which are echoed in multiple re-territorialisations of museums worldwide. First, was the *Te Maori* exhibition, which toured Aotearoa/New Zealand's major cities as well as several cities in the United States through the 1980s. Two key things happened during this exhibition: Māori insisted on providing openings, the support of elders and guided tours of the exhibition, and the elders challenged the museum to tour the *taonga*[8] in their *marae* communities (Tapsell 2015: 267). However, it wasn't until 20 years after this challenge that the Auckland museum were willing to recognise *marae* communities as coproducers of the touring exhibition (Tapsell 2015: 267). Finally, in 2001, the *Ko Tawa* exhibition project was launched. *Ko Tawa* sought to include Māori voices at numerous points throughout the curatorial process. Important to note is that the inclusion of these voices affected other components on a temporal scale that exceeded the exhibition itself. Alongside the development of the exhibition was the bringing together of a 'Māori Values Team', who, over a six-year period gave regular tutorial sessions to museum volunteers, staff and the museum board in order to assist in an institution-wide understanding of 'tribally informed perspectives' of *taonga* (Tapsell 2015: 264). The overarching curatorial strategy in the research phase of *Ko Tawa* was to reconnect the *taonga* to their genealogically layered narratives in a way that included the values and ideologies of Māori gift-giving, and tribal authority. This was a process seen to be 'indigenous knowledge-centred rather than driven by a museum's aesthetic, ethnological or political agenda' (Tapsell 2015: 266).

Over these years, the Māori Values Team's work was translated into the priorities of the Auckland Museum, evidenced in the changed 'vision, mission and values' statement articulated in the Auckland Museum Annual Plan 2003–2004. Then, in 2003–2004, the vision statement is 'To be a source of inspiration to our communities', while the mission statement is 'Collect and care for our communities' treasures in order to tell object-based stories in a way that stimulates mind and spirit' (AWMM Annual Report 2003–2004). Prior to this, the vision and mission statement read quite differently, with no mention of communities.

From 1997 (when the vision, mission, and values statement was first introduced to the Annual Report) to 2002, the statement expressed that the role of the museum included 'being the heart of our culture', 'caring for treasures', performing a role of 'guardianship' to these treasures, 'gathering knowledge:

studying and interpreting our heritage and environment through our treasures' and (only from the year 2000) 'respect for the treaty of Waitangi' (AWMM Annual Report 1997 to 1998, 2000 to 2001, 2002–2003). As a result of pressure from the *Tuamata-a-Iwi*[9] one Māori exhibition annually was established as a performance indicator by the Auckland Museum (Tapsell 2015: 268). This led to a modest exhibition budget and a designated 'small pictorial gallery' at the rear of the museum from 2004.

Re-territorialising a museum assemblage from the normative is no small task, and in the case of the Auckland Museum, required a concerted effort from several resource components working together. One area of major contention in the *Ko Tawa* case was the touring of *taonga* through *marae*. Tapsell recalls how in late 2004, the Auckland Museum's director, financial controller and members of the trust board froze the project, concerned that this defied museum policy standard museum procedure. After convincing the management level of the museum that conservation and care measures would not be compromised, and also that the exhibition would fulfil policy requirements to engage source communities, the project was once again given the go-ahead (Tapsell 2015: 272–273). The values of 'guardianship' espoused in the earlier museum mission, and along with those the perception of ownership and authority, required not only a change in the written statement but the sustained effort of staff in exercising an expressive role. This of course could not have been achieved without other relational components in alignment (government and museum policy, the source communities and the additional budget provided by private sponsorship).

In the case of the Auckland Museum, the components at play are the *taonga*, various stakeholders (predominantly museum professionals, academics, and source communities), and policy. The relational quality is the collective formed by the Māori Values Team, their training programmes, and the consequent effect on internal museum priorities, which has since affected curatorial strategy and exhibition programming. Tapsell (2015: 268) describes the process:

> At least 50 of the 247 taonga carried powerful enough narratives to captivate our target audiences and these became the *Ko Tawa* shortlist. Thereafter, we departed from objective selection based on aesthetic, ethnological or any other previously employed museological process, instead engaging *whakapapa*– a value system based on the Maori genealogical ordering of the universe out of which *taonga* originated– to make our selection.

As written exhibition labels are at odds with the mnemonic oral histories of the Māori, and glass display cabinets are seen as a violation to the living ancestral spirits of *taonga*, the exhibition was designed with these traditional display components deliberately omitted.[10] While the living elders of the source communities were referred to as co-producers through this exhibition, their capacity to exercise relations to the curation process was constrained, as evidenced by the first half of Tapsell's statement above. Further, the *kaiarahi* (guiding hosts) – who were members of local tribes and in many instances' direct descendants from the *taonga* – were 'trained' by the museum team, 'receiving museum-associated *Ko Tawa* knowledge' to be integrated into their own experiences (Tapsell 2015: 274). Numerous stakeholders, opinions, and values coalesce in responsive museums. According to Simon Knell (2019), the lesson we receive from Aotearoa/New Zealand is that museums and their communities much 'share a vision of change'. For those coming from a colonial heritage or system of education, this necessitates a relinquishing of former ways of doing things. It also requires a sense of responsibility and ethics, as well as a flexibility to recognise that, as an entanglement of lived relationships, processes will need to remain open to negotiation.

The desire to include a multiplicity of voices and do justice to both the cultural heritage objects and their source communities is evident in the responsive museum assemblage. And yet, the notion that these source communities need to be trained to reflect museum knowledge, that the final custodianship of the objects rests within the museums conservation and care policies, and that each exhibition requires educative material alongside it shows the constraints placed on many components. Ultimately, there remains a precarious balance between 'professional knowledge' and 'community knowledge'. However, it is the capacity for the components that make up these two facets to affect back on the assemblage whole – through processes of negotiation – that is key to the responsive assemblage. This is what distinguishes a 'formal' responsiveness, as articulated through Ang's (2015) research, from an actual responsiveness, as seen here. In a 2009 interview with McCarthy (2019: 47), Rhonda Paku (Manager Iwi Development at Te Papa) underscored the attempts to incorporate structures of institutional support to allow Māori communities to make decisions around the care of their *taonga*. She goes on to note that this practice is about 'utilising the best of both worlds' when it comes to the combination of Indigenous knowledge and museum skills. Kimberly Christen (2015) articulates this duality when she emphasises how indigenous curatorial practices tend to accommodate other knowledge, even while privileging a source communities' knowledge. Knowledge hybridity is evident in the art exhibition at Te Papa, in which the intersections of Māori and Pākehā cultures play both material and expressive roles through their display. One room is thematically devoted to cultural appropriation, with signage asking 'What is appropriation in art? When is it sampling, reference, homage? When is it theft?'. Within this room is a work by Francis Upritchard *Untitled* (2002–2003), accompanied by the following text:

> The head in this case is part of Francis Upritchard's series of so-called Pākehā shrunken heads. The works recall the trade in the 1800s of *toi moko* (tattooed Māori preserved heads) and *kōiwi tangata* (Māori skeletal

remains) between private collectors, museums, and universities. The trade of ancestral remains is a disturbing aspect of New Zealand's history, and the collusion of various parties in the exchange sits uncomfortably today.

This display, in the context of the wider assemblage, can be read as symbolic of Te Papa as a responsive museum. It holds a meta-narrative of what it is to balance different cultures, historical perspectives and voices. The lack of a distinct 'answer' for reading this part of the exhibition is a recognition of the tension, conflict, questioning and negotiation that is part and parcel of being responsive. The open-endedness of a responsive process is made evident in this alignment of curatorial strategy and visitor experience. Responsive museums can take on vastly different exhibition strategies, as the needs of various constituents are different depending on the geographical location and cultural context of the museum. The community groups and therefore the practices at Te Papa are unlike those at MG. However, through all the entanglements and interactions between components at each museum, two principles emerge that affirm the responsive assemblage as a common notion. The first is that constituents and community groups are not only represented within the museum but afforded a greater capacity to affect back on the assemblage through their presence in the museum. The second is that the responsive museum is made up of interactions between community and professional authority.

Notes

1 For the third phase of institutional critique, see chapter six.
2 This extends to interventions by artists such as Andrea Fraser, Fred Wilson, and Christian Philip Müller, who 'were concerned with exploring the social and political agendas concealed behind the museum's supposedly neutral façade' (Putnam 2009: 31).
3 Slowness may be part and parcel of engagement with community, but it is also a point of contention. According to McCarthy; 'When I visit museums in Australia, talk to staff, and attend professional gathering and conferences, what is apparent to me is the bitter resentment among young Indigenous professionals at the slow pace of change' (McCarthy 2019: 44).
4 'Iwi' is used throughout this chapter as the official term for a Māori tribe.
5 'When the so-called 'Balkan migratory route' expanded to Slovenia's state borders, many cultural institutions as well as individuals kept asking themselves how to act. Moderna Galerija saw its role in establishing a discourse that would fight against racial prejudice, would recognize existing initiatives, and reflect on the possibilities of building a common solidarity network' (Železnik 2018: 57). See also Igor Španjol's (2018: 257–259) reflection on MG's work in the 1990s, with curators collecting work for a (still not realised) museum of contemporary art in Sarajevo in order to show solidarity with Bosnia-Herzegovina following the war in the former Yugoslavia.
6 This is also echoed on the MG website. In articulating the museum's history, the site states; 'In the crucial period of the 1990s, Moderna galerija refused to become a postmodern museum of sensations and intense experiences; on the threshold of

the new millennium it fairly clearly developed the concept of an art museum that advocates the plurality of narratives and priorities of local spaces that intend to enter equal dialogues with other spaces only with their own symbolic capital' (MG + MSUM Website: Visions 2019).

7 A meeting ground that belongs to a particular iwi (tribe), hapū (sub-tribe), or whanau (family).

8 A simplified definition of the Māori *taonga* is 'cultural treasures', but within them are the ancestral spirits of the *marae* communities from which they originate.

9 The legislated Maori Advisory Committee under the Auckland Museum's 1996 Amendment Act.

10 There was, however, a 'take-home "exhibition labels" booklet' (Tapsell 2015: 273).

References

Ang, Ien (2015). 'Change and Continuity: Art Museums and the Reproduction of Art Museumness'. A. Witcomb and K. Message (eds.) *The International Handbooks of Museum Studies: Museum Theory*. Cambridge, MA/Oxford: Wiley Blackwell. Pp. 211–232.

AWMM Annual Report 1997 to 1998 Auckland Museum Annual Report Archive. https://annualreportarchive.aucklandmuseum.com/report/aim_ann_report_19961997/, last accessed 10 February 2017.

AWMM Annual Report 2000 to 2001 Auckland Museum Annual Report Archive. https://annualreportarchive.aucklandmuseum.com/report/aim_ann_report_2000–2001/, last accessed 10 February 2017.

AWMM Annual Report 2002–2003 Auckland Museum Annual Report Archive. https://archive.org/details/AucklandMuseumAnnualReport2002–2003, last accessed 10 February 2017.

AWMM Annual Report 2003–2004 Auckland Museum Annual Report Archive. https://annualreportarchive.aucklandmuseum.com/report/aim_ann_report_2003–2004/, last accessed 10 February 2017.

Bennett, Tony (2013). *Making Culture, Changing Society*. London: Routledge.

Byrne, John, Elinor Morgan, November Paynter, Aida Sánchez de Serdio, Adela Železnik (eds.) (2018). *The Constituent Museum: Constellations of Knowledge, Politics and Mediation*. Amsterdam: Valiz.

Christen, Kimberly (2015). 'On Not Looking: Economies of Visuality in Digital Museums'. A.E. Coombes and R.B. Phillips (eds.) *The International Handbooks of Museum Studies: Museum Transformations*. Cambridge, MA/Oxford: Wiley Blackwell. Pp. 365–386.

Crooke, Elizabeth (2015). 'The "Active Museum": How Concern with Community Transformed the Museum'. C. McCarthy (ed.) *The International Handbooks of Museum Studies: Museum Practice*. Cambridge, MA/Oxford: Wiley Blackwell. Pp. 481–502.

de Jong, Steffi. (2015). 'Mediatized Memory: Video Testimonies in Museums'. M. Henning (ed.) *The International Handbooks of Museum Studies: Museum Media*. Cambridge, MA/Oxford: Wiley Blackwell. Pp. 69–94.

Every Man is a Curator. (2007). Moderna Galerija, Ljubljana. Exhibition.

Karp, Ivan and Corinne A. Kratz (2015). 'The Interrogative Museum'. R.A. Silverman (ed.) *Museum as Process: Translating Local and Global Knowledges*. London/New York: Routledge. Pp. 279–298.

Knell, Simon (2019). *The Contemporary Museum: Shaping Museums for the Global Now*. London/New York: Routledge.

Lang, Caroline, John Reeve and Vicky Woollard (2006). *The Responsive Museum: Working with Audiences in the Twenty-First Century*. London/New York: Routledge.

Lynch, Bernadette (2011). *Whose Cake is it Anyway?* London: Paul Hamlyn Foundation.

Marstine, Janet (2006). *New Museum Theory and Practice: An Introduction*. Oxford: Blackwell.

McCarthy, Conal (2019). 'Indigenisation: Reconceptualising Museology'. S. Knell (ed.) *The Contemporary Museum: Shaping Museums for the Global Now*. London/New York: Routledge. Pp. 37–54.

McSweeney, Kayte and Jen Kavanagh (2016). *Museum Participation: New Directions for Audience Collaboration*. Edinburgh, UK: MuseumsEtc.

MG+MSUM: Collaborations. https://www.mg-lj.si/en/about-us/848/collaborations/, last accessed 23 March 2019.

MG+MSUM: Vision. https://www.mg-lj.si/en/about-us/901/mgmsum-vision/, last accessed 23 March 2019.

New Zealand Ministry for Culture and Heritage. https://www.mch.govt.nz/what-wedo/cultural sector-overviews/cultural-policy-new-zealand/2-administrativeand-institutional, last accessed 3 March 2017.

Piškur, Bojana (2018). 'Possibilities for Emancipation'. J. Byrne, E. Morgan, N. Paynter, A. Sánchez de Serdio and A. Železnik (eds.) *The Constituent Museum: Constellations of Knowledge, Politics and Mediation*. Amsterdam: Valiz. Pp. 174–177.

Pogačar Podgornik, Tjaša (2018). 'Vsak Človek Je Kustos!/Jeder Mensch IST Ein Kurator!'. J. Byrne, E. Morgan, N. Paytner, A. Sánchez de Serdio and A. Železnik (eds.) *The Constituent Museum: Constellations of Knowledge, Politics and Mediation*. Amsterdam: Valiz. Pp. 274–277.

Pollock, Griselda (2007). 'Un-Framing the Modern: Critical Space/Public Possibility'. G. Pollock and J. Zemans (eds.) *Museums After Modernism: Strategies of Engagement*. MA/Oxford/Victoria: Blackwell. Pp. 1–39.

Putnam, James (2009/2001). *Art and Artifact: The Museum as Medium*. London: Thames and Hudson.

Raunig, Gerald (2009). 'Instituent Practices: Fleeing, Instituting, Transforming'. G. Raunig and G. Ray (eds.) *Art and Contemporary Critical Practice: Reinventing Institutional Critique*. London: MayFlyBooks. Pp. 3–12.

Sandell, Richard (2016). *Museums, Moralities and Human Rights*. London/New York: Routledge.

Sandell, Richard (2019). 'Disability: Museums and Our Understandings of Difference'. S. Knell (ed.) *The Contemporary Museum: Shaping Museums for the Global Now*. London/New York: Routledge. Pp. 169–184.

Silverman, Raymond A. (2015). *Museum as Process: Translating Local and Global Knowledges*. London/New York: Routledge.

Španjol, Igor. (2018). 'Solidarity'. J. Byrne, E. Morgan, N. Paynter, A. Sánchez de Serdio, A. Železnik (eds.). *The Constituent Museum: Constellations of Knowledge, Politics and Mediation*. Amsterdam: Valiz. Pp. 256–259.

Tapsell, Paul (2015). 'Ko Tawa: Where are the Glass Cabinets?'. R.A. Silverman (ed.) *Museum as Process: Translating Local and Global Knowledges*. London/New York: Routledge. Pp. 262–278.

Te Papa (2018) 'Annual Report 2017–18'. *Museum of New Zealand Te Papa Tongarewa*. https://www.tepapa.govt.nz/sites/default/files/te_papa_annual_report_2017–18_0. pdf, last accessed 11 January 2019.

Thomas, Nicholas (2016). *The Return of Curiosity: What Museums are Good For in the 21st Century*. London: Reaktion Books.

Vergo, Peter (1989). *The New Museology*. London: Reaktion Books.

Witcomb, Andrea (2003). *Re-Imagining the Museum: Beyond the Mausoleum*. London/ New York: Routledge.

Witcomb, Andrea (2015). 'Cultural Pedagogies in the Museum'. M. Watkins, G. Noble and C Driscoll (eds.) *Cultural Pedagogies and Human Conduct*. London/New York: Routledge.

Železnik, Adela. (2018). 'New communities of Migrants.' J. Byrne, E. Morgan, N. Paynter, A. Sánchez de Serdio, A. Železnik (eds.). *The Constituent Museum: Constellations of Knowledge, Politics and Mediation*. Amsterdam: Valiz. Pp. 56–59.

5   The Affective Museum

Atmospherics, Aesthesis, and the Sensorial

The affective common notion highlights museum practices that focus on sensorial and immersive experience, haptic engagement, ambient aesthetics, and museum atmospherics. In museology, atmospherics is predominantly approached in two ways. The first is through tracing the overlaps and impacts of marketing practices and the experience/entertainment economy in the museum. Brigitte Biehl-Missal and Dirk vom Lehn (2015) write on atmosphere and aesthetics in museums from a critical marketing perspective. They find that 'strategies' of atmosphere are utilised in museums to attract the wider public, but that these are often perceived as a 'technique to feed consumerism in the disguise of widening access' (Biehl-Missal and vom Lehn 2015: 253). However, they can also 'constitute a real social power because they influence people via bodily and sensual perception' (Biehl-Missal and vom Lehn 2015: 253). In other words, it is not through the components themselves, but through their relations that atmosphere is perceived as invoking consumer ideology or social ideology.

The second is through a more general concept of aesthesis, or the sensual perception of reality.[1] In considering both of these approaches, atmospherics is an area that all museum assemblages encapsulate. However, in the affective assemblage, museum practices are produced through the prioritisation of atmospheric aesthesis, which is exercised by the roles of the assemblage components. While the visitor experiences affect as an embodied response to a stimulus in every museum, the affective museum is territorialised by positioning pre-rational engagement at the core of its practice. The visitor's personal experience and their interaction with the materiality of the museum is given precedence over information and traditional pedagogy. We need to distinguish between museums that employ affective resources as a corporatist strategy (promoting consumption and treating the viewer as a consumer), and museums that focus on how we learn (about ourselves, about others, about the world) through embodied experience. Visitor interactivity and engagement occur across all museums (with varying capacities and afforded roles). The ambient space and atmospherics of the affective museum encourages reflexive and participative modalities.

DOI: 10.4324/9781003393719-6

While affective practices have been explored through two lens' of consumerism and aesthesis, it is the latter that is most relevant for this assemblage. In this respect, we can turn to the artistic practices explored in Bourriaud's (1998) *relational aesthetics*. From Bourriaud's stance, interactive and relational concepts defined art of the 1990s. Through this decade, artworks that involved participatory elements in order to become 'activated', in a type of co-production, became popularised, and made (or forced) their way into exhibition spaces. These kinds of works were seen to be a response to the 'spectacle' of modernity, aiming to produce sets of interactions that combatted the positioning of individual as consumer, offering participation as a means to gain insight into social relations.

Bourriaud's (1998) relational aesthetics is a response to a society where behaviour and relations are mediated through commodity rather than 'directly experienced'. It is interesting to consider the relationship between this argument and the affective museum assemblage. On the one hand, the affective museum privileges the lived, 'directly experienced' engagement with objects and space. On the other hand, these immersive environments are some of the most highly mediated (and in addition, some of the most circulated images online). Nonetheless, as Antony Jackson and Jenny Kidd have argued, visits to museums are increasingly about the experience rather than the objects (2012: 2).

The turn towards subject–object relations had ramifications for the development of the affective museum as a common notion. If we look to Sandra Dudley's work around museum objects (2010), we see that the physicality of an object holds a capacity to affect, playing a vital role in the visitors embodied experience of the museum. She notes that while the experience of the museum object still exists in relation to the informational and socio-cultural inscriptions that often accompany it, the materiality of the object is also experienced in a different set of relations, through the object–subject interaction. The materiality of museums creates a 'dynamic interaction' by bringing together physical forms and sensory experiences (Dudley 2010: 7–8).

With focus on the sensory and the immersive in contemporary museums, we can begin to note the importance of reverie and imagination in the visitor experience of affective museums. If we consider that the way that we write about museums also contains the capacity to affect back on the assemblage, it is important to note here the correlation between experiential, phenomenological, and embodied accounts of museum practice and the understanding of the affective assemblage. The work of Andrea Witcomb (2013) on museums and affect has been pivotal in recognising the aesthetic entanglements that emerge when the sensorial and embodied interact with the material and spatial. This entanglement produces meaning through sense-making as intuitive and felt, shifting away from the rationalising discourse of information-based content. A reflexive positioning of the work of academics as one component in relation to others within the museum indicates the contributing role of museum scholars in forming the way we perceive an affective museum. As visitor studies began to extend beyond the quantitative outcome surveys aiming to measure a wide-scale social and educative value, phenomenological enquiry began to emerge as a trend in the study of museums visitors (Radywyl 2008; Radywyl et al 2015; Baker 2010; Grewcock 2014). Phenomenological accounts serve to territorialise the assemblage as affective. This kind of focus on embodied experience highlighted the potentiality of affect in museum practice.

To explore the way museum components come together to form an affective common notion, I have drawn on the Lee Ufan Museum, part of the Benesse Art Site Naoshima in Japan, as well as Sammlung Boros in Berlin.[2] Each have a particular focus on the importance of scenography – through their architecture, relationship with the museum's immediate environment, and the privileging of the aesthetic experience (sensing as sense-making) over the rational-didactic. Conversely, in assessing how affective common notions can be re-territorialised, I turn to the Museo nazionale delle arti del XXI secolo (MAXXI) in Rome, and the Centro de Arte Contemporânea Inhotim (Inhotim) in Brazil. Both MAXXI and Inhotim are valuable indicators of how museum assemblages do not operate along a linear historical trajectory beginning with the normative and shifting into other common notions.

Affective Museum Priorities

We can summarise the affective museum's priorities as the following interrelated concepts; a return to wonder, visitor participation, sensory experience, and immersion. Both responsive and affective museum assemblages prioritise visitors. A crucial point to make here is that the practices of the responsive museum position the visitor within a sense of a collective, e.g. 'the public' or 'constituents', while affective museum practices indicate that the visitor is formed as 'individual' and positioned only as part of a collective within the space of the museum. We can connect to the words of John Berger (1972) in order to consider how sensory experiences came to be prioritised within the affective museum:

> If the new language of images were used differently, it would, through its use, confer a new kind of power. Within it we could begin to define our experiences more precisely in areas where words are inadequate. (Seeing comes before words.) Not only personal experience, but also the essential historical experience of our relation to the past: that is to say the experience of seeking to give meaning to our lives, of trying to understand the history of which we can become the active agents.
>
> (Berger 1972 [2008]: 33)

A 'new language of images' (which in this case include the lighting, sound, and the other resources forming the 'ambient cues' of the affective museum) 'activates' agency in museum visitor relations. As Natalia Radywyl (2008) highlights in her study of the Australian Centre for the Moving Image (ACMI), visitor movement is determined by affective cues (e.g. lighting) that act as 'navigational suggestions'. This heightens the role of sensory perception in the visitors experience of the exhibition space. In an immersive museum experience, one cannot separate the different components of the museum. The notion of a wholistic experience is not a new one. Seen to stem from Ludwig Mies van Der Rohe's design proposal *Museum for a Small City*, through Europe in the 1950s and 1960s there was a growing trend in considering the impact of architecture and spatiality on the reception of art. The focus on the environmental surroundings, alongside additional public programming and spaces for the museum, established the idea of the museum as a *Gesamtkunstwerk*, 'the idea of the museum as a whole work of art' (Tzortzi 2015: 26), which includes not only the collections but the building itself. Foregrounding the immersive associations of the *Gesamtkunstwerk*, the connections the visitor makes within the affective museum can only be understood within the context of the environment and atmosphere of the space. The Benesse Art Site Naoshima emphasises a learning experience that is focused on 'feeling', rather than traditional informational knowledge. This type of learning process is dependent on the idea that the museum experience is bound not to the physical structure of the museum but rather to the spaces and their surrounding environment. The site-specificity of the museums' architecture is seen throughout with architect Tadao Ando submerging and integrating the structures into the landscape. Their mission states:

> Our fundamental aim is to create significant spaces by bringing contemporary art and architecture in resonance with the pristine nature of the Seto Inland Sea, a landscape with a rich cultural and historical fabric. Through contacts with art and nature, sceneries and inhabitants of the Seto Inland Sea region, we seek to inspire visitors to reflect on the meaning of Benesse's motto- Well-Being.
>
> (Benesse Art Site n.d.)

The affective museum prioritises the visitor–environment relationship. This priority is then territorialised through resource components, which come together in (often highly staged) conditions in order to forge a sensory relation and create a sense of atmosphere perceptible to the museum visitor.

Affective Museum Resources

We have seen many expressive resources within normative (see Chapter 3) and responsive (see Chapter 4) museums (particularly in regard to directional signage and interpretative text). The affective assemblage takes a stronger focus on the expressive qualities of material resources, such as architecture, sound, light, and objects. The notable absence of additional interpretative material is a common feature of the affective museum assemblage. Across the Lee Ufan Museum and Sammlung Boros, there are no wall placards. As a result, the visitor is inclined to draw on other resources in order to interpret the exhibition, the relationship between the museum architecture, lighting, sound, and artworks/objects.

It is through staging the environment that the affective museum develops a participatory experience. Ambient cues, such as music, scent, lighting, and temperature are the stimuli through which the visitors experience is shaped. Where other museum practices are ocular-centric, the affective museum engages full sensory capabilities. When we consider the sensual perception of reality, an ocular centric focus becomes limiting. The affective assemblage, then, does not privilege the visual in terms of connecting it with a discourse of rational spectatorship. The affective assemblage moves the visitor modality to one of participation and immersion.

Nowadays many museums have touch exhibitions, as well as tactile educational provisions and participatory art exhibitions offering visitors points of interaction, or in some cases, even production. Touching vs. not touching is just one demonstration of the ways in which sensory practices within museums differ. Touch is now understood as a valuable sensory modality in many museum spaces. In this respect, the term 'haptics', taken from discussion around performance and participatory art, is used in order to account for a multiplicity of sensory modalities in relation to touch. These include, among other examples of active touch, perceptions of vibration, pressure, temperature, pain, balance, grip, and texture (Candlin 2010: 5). Often haptic interactions in the museum are written about in relation to digital media interfaces (Kidd 2014). However, in normative museums, digital interactives like Graphic User Interfaces (GUIs) tend to act in the capacity of providing additional information to strengthen the pre-existing narrative set out by the museum. While they engage touch and sound in addition to vision, they do not encourage an imaginative, sensorial, *pre-rational* response, separating this practice from affective practices. In responsive museums, the focus tends to be about using the technological affordances of digital media to increase access and a multiplicity of voices, or to present exhibits in a 'documentary' style, to fortify the legitimacy of community sources. The use of digital interactives in the museum is not synonymous with an affective assemblage. Rather, it is a more complex set of practices between the other mediated components of the space that again determine how the museums common notion comes to form an affective assemblage. Radywyl (2008) explores this within the hyper-mediatised environment of ACMI. However, there is also a point to be made that in many cases – of all the museum assemblages – affective assemblages have the least digital interactives at the physical site of the museum. The two museums taken as case studies in this chapter do not have any GUIs. Photography is explicitly banned inside these spaces. Not only is there an absence of digital interactives in the space, the visitor is also discouraged from experiencing the museum through the lens of their camera or screen of their smartphone. This creates spaces of reverie, a strikingly involved engagement that shifts the 'art-worshipful' premise of the normative common notion to a reverence of space and embodiment in the affective.

In addition to the renewed interest in tactility within certain institutions, we see the pull towards aural experiences. The sonic and sound art are brought into the museum as part of exhibitions or as installations themselves in a push towards 'immersive' exhibition environments. Rupert Cox explores the use of sound in the museum, looking at several museum sound installations to explore 'the modes of relational and affective sociality that are engendered by sound in the museum' (Cox 2015: 216). While sound is rife in all museum spaces – murmuring, footsteps – sound in normative museums is limited and carefully managed so as to not detract from the relationship between 'spectator' and object. However, in affective museum spaces, sensory components like sound are considered to contribute to the experience of the space. Cox (2015: 227) writes that the 'ambiguity of sound' can act as a navigational suggestion, pulling the focus away from the ocular-centric, and creating a different set of spatial relations for visitors. The extra material and expressive roles afforded to these resources in the staging of the museum destabilise the primacy of vision that has accompanied the history of aesthetic judgment and institutional value systems. In Sammlung Boros, many of the installations work with sound so that visitors are confronted with various, overlapping sounds creating a soundscape through the bunker's five floors. However, one can only visit the Sammlung as part of a guided tour and as such, the lack of wall cards does not necessarily mean a lack of interpretative material. Much of the tour takes a focus on the architecture of the building, lending credence to the idea of an immersive experience. Holding a similar principle, though with a different affective aim, the website introduction for the Lee Ufan Museum reads:

> Located in a gentle valley surrounded by hills and the ocean, the museum offers a tranquil space where nature, architecture and art come in resonance with each other, inviting to peaceful and quiet contemplation, in a society overflowing with material goods.
>
> (Benesse Art Site: Lee Ufan Museum n.d.)

The emphasis on environment and feeling ('well-being', 'tranquil space', 'peaceful and quiet contemplation'), and the noted synergy between 'nature, architecture and art', serve to territorialise Lee Ufan Museum as affective. The site continues with 'The floor plan with rectangular and triangular spaces arranged across this valley which leads to the sea brings a rhythm to the architecture'. In the Lee Ufan Museum, before one has even entered the threshold, the visitor must walk through a corridor of vast concrete walls, which block out everything apart from a strip of sky above. Once in the museum, the majority of the rooms have no windows, and deeply recessed skylights are utilised to create a nuanced play of light and shadow through the exhibition spaces. The Sammlung Boros building, having started its life as a war bunker, is a fortress from the outside world. This has had a great flow-on effect for other components to exercise their role. It is the fire regulations of the building that stipulate group size, and the architecture of the building has presented a lot of difficulties as it is windowless. This impacts on other components within the museum. Boros has previously stated:

> [T]he works often acquire another kind of power in these windowless cells! After one and a half hours in this series of chambers, people are exhausted when they leave. These are extreme conditions – it's an encounter with the self, and perhaps even a type of torture. The tour is a kind of pilgrimage.
> (Boros in Hohmann 2013: 28)

There is a nice historical link to be made here. Art historian Carol Duncan parallels the architecture of donor museums to mausolea, sepulchers and churches or temples, claiming this is due to the popular interpretation of art galleries as 'sacred spaces' through the eighteenth and nineteenth centuries (Duncan 1995: 83). Having illustrated the way in which the affective assemblage lends itself to interactions that are simultaneously performative/participatory and sacred (though not necessarily always 'untouchable' in the literal or metaphoric sense), we find a surprising answer to this question. Performative and participatory approaches, when in conjunction with components that create an ambient aesthetics, can lend themselves to a perception of the museum as a sacred realm to be 'revered'.

Affective Museum Publics

In the affective museum, individual subjectivity is acknowledged as a legitimate experience of the museum space. The affective assemblage interacts with the visitor component primarily as an individual subject, and as a collective only in within the physicality of the museum site. This has implications for the way in which the 'public' is realised in a present tense. For example, in response to a question about why Sammlung Boros is housed in the middle of Berlin, rather than in a country estate, owner–collector Christian Boros said that he wants to be a part of what is happening, that he is a 'part of the present' (Boros in Lapp 2019). The duality, of 'presence' and 'present' mirrors what I established as the foundation of affect; an embodied, felt response. It occurs only as a moment of engagement, existing only in the present via a presence. By bringing scenography-focused components together in a space with the aim of creating immersive, atmospheric relations, the affective assemblage's 'public' are the body of people sharing a spatiotemporal moment in the museum. Other components playing into this are the banning of photographs and the lack of wall placards, the first which creates a barrier between the individual and the present moment (one cannot 'capture' an atmosphere for later) and the second, which can be seen to encourage a rational response to the works in the space.

Boros also creates a connection between his idea of 'publics' and the environment by saying, 'When someone comes to Berlin, all synapses are put on receive. There are curious people here, and it's fun to share something with curious people' (Boros in Lapp 2019). We see curiosity invoked as a relational interaction between visitors and other components in the affective assemblage. Boros also highlights a crucial feature of how visitor components come together within the affective common notion to shape the overarching museum experience. In terms of the interplay between individual visitors and collective experience, each of my visitations to Sammlung Boros has been vastly different. In July 2016, the tour guide encourages our group to squeeze through artist Michael Sailstorfer's *Himmel, Berlin* (2012), a collection of large, half-inflated, twisted black tubes protrudes from a corner room into an adjoining doorway. An older visitor moves through the work with his eyes closed, the rubber textures pushing on him from every angle. Moments later, he recounts how, in the early 1990s, he had been to a queer rubber-fetish night at the Bunker, back when it was used as an illegal club space for techno music and sex/fetish parties. Moving through the artwork in this way had taken him back to that last time he was in the building, decades earlier. The rest of the group spends some additional time in the artwork, eyes closed and sly smiles on their faces. This fresh insight and consequent immersive and haptic experience create a sense of connection – with each other, with the artwork, and with the building through time.

By the time I visit again in July 2018, there is a new rotation of artworks, a new guide, a new group going through the space with me. The dynamic is entirely different with this new assemblage, largely due to the visitor component. Previously, a sense of conviviality was a constitutive part of the visitation experience. This group is quiet, listens attentively to the words of the guide, following him quickly and cautiously from room to room, without lingering on. We arrive at Paulo Nazareth's work *Arma Branca* (2013), which invites you to make your own paper print of the work using provided ink and stamps. Only I and one other woman partake, and we do so in silence.

These visitations shed light on the dynamics between visitors that shape the visitor experience in the moment of presence. It should come as no surprise that sociality and companionship shape our visitor experience. These two experiences set in relation to one another show that, regardless of individual subjectivities, components in the museum can work towards particular affects that become a shared experience for visitors. This was also found to be the case in the visual art ethnography project conducted by Lydia Nakashima Degarrod (2010). She found that 'objects tend to create ambiguous meanings which relate to the body or the senses', in turn forging more personal and emotional reactions (Nakashima Degarrod 2010: 138–139).

With the prioritisation of visitors in both responsive and affective assemblages, value is attributed to both engagement and participation. However, once again, we see that the way components exercise their roles in the affective museum creates a different set of processes and practices around engagement and participation. A prioritisation of resources that contribute to sensory experience, through sound, light, and other technologies, affords visitors the opportunity to exercise a different set of relations in the museum space. As Radywyl found:

> Visitors' interaction with technology-based art enables knowledge to circulate through cognitive processes of self-enquiry, as visitors set their own boundaries for interpretation according to the parameters of their perception. In doing so they create a new interrogatory space which challenges the traditional circulation of knowledge in the museum.
>
> (Radywyl 2008: 120)

Radywyl also notes that in one visitor interview, the interviewee expressed that a more educative exhibit included an explanation of the technology, making the processes of the technological operations transparent so that 'it's an educational process, as well as an arts process' (Radywyl 2008: 121). This indicates the internalisation of normative processes, which would 'undermine the conditions of ambiguity' (Radywyl 2008: 122) in a museum that aims to foreground the sensory, embodied, and atmospheric experience. This assertion is indicative of a territorialising relation in the affective museum assemblage. It also positions the affective common notion as one wherein visitor engagement is deliberately more highly individualised/individuated.

Both Degarrod's and Radywyl's findings align with my experiences of Sammlung Boros. The first experience illustrates that when many of the resource components traditionally found in museums are absent, the visitor is given a heightened expressive capacity in engaging with other components of the museum. It serves as a reminder of what Dudley posited when she wrote of the museum visitation that 'I may add other sensory elements to the visual even if they have to be imagined, intuited or remembered' (2010: 9). In the second visit, the 'buffer' of the guide leads me back to the safety zone of a normative interaction. The two visitations in relation to each other highlight the capacity for the visitor component to affect back on the assemblage whole. If the collective of visitors are open to the affective interpretations of the space and share in expressing the embodied sensations that the exhibition arouses, they contribute to an affective territorialisation. This was my first experience of the Bunker. On the other hand, if the collective interacts with the other components in another way, normative relations emerge, and the museum is momentarily held as a normative common notion.

There is an ambiguity to the experience of affective museums. Resource components forming ambient cues – lighting, architecture – come together to form a feeling. This is at odds with the normative and responsive assemblages, where the curatorial hand is overt rather than ambient, and the interpretative material comes in written form. This affords the object/artwork components of the museum a greater capacity to affect, in the double sense of the word. Unlike the normative or responsive museum assemblages, the affective museum emphasises forms of self-exploratory navigation and moving from the ontology of knowing to the ontology of feeling. The affective museum is characterised through a prioritisation of environment, atmospherics, and sensorial experience. It is interesting to note that, of the museums I have visited, those that may be territorialised as an affective common notion are all privately funded. This adds credence to the idea that in publicly funded museums are implicated in a public service role that sees education as didactic, as opposed to learning through embodied sensing and feeling.

Affective Museum Processes

The following narrative is an observation of how components relations form an atmospheric presence that territorialises the affective museum. I turn to my visitation of Lee Ufan Museum in August of 2015 in order to explore how museum components interact to form an affective assemblage.

The Lee Ufan museum is located in a small, naturally formed basin, with the museum built into the hillside behind and virtually invisible from the outside, save for a minimalistic concrete wall and courtyard. Two boulders are set near each other on the grass before the courtyard, with a dark, rectangular slab acting as a wall between them. Another boulder, and several trees appearing to grow seamlessly from the stone ground, are positioned in the courtyard. Together, it provides a soft transition between nature and the manmade. Walking into the entrance, concrete walls tower over you, the sky above turned into a slit of blue tinged with a whisper of cloud, like a singular brushstroke. Making a U-shape one follows the sky until reaching an automatic sliding door with a small foyer and reception desk. The staff member quietly points to their left, into the gallery space.

Moving through the space it is hushed and minimal, a mirror to the works of Lee Ufan housed within. The biggest room holds large canvases, Ufan's paintings occupy each of the walls. They exist, uninterrupted, without descriptive plaques beside them. A *wabi-sabi* rock placed on a square of dark reflective material marks the centre of the room, performing the part of a sculptural piece found in other museums. Other visitors follow the desire line of the four walls, drifting from one work to the next in a systematic fashion. Appearing to be lit by a single light, a darkened hallway to the side offers another stone, its shadow a video projection on the ground. Throughout, an interplay of stone, of reflective squares and rectangles, wood and concrete, of minimal lighting and echoed lines, shape the museum.

Shoes are taken off to enter the final exhibition room. This room, furthest from the entrance, presents as an empty square, with simple vase-like shapes painted directly onto each wall and an opening in the ceiling giving view to the sky. The room is remarkably silent, though during the time I am there, I am always joined by at least several other individuals as visitors came and went. Most notably, as people come into the room they – without direction – immediately sit or lay down on the floor and gaze either at the basic vase design on the wall or up through to the sky. This impromptu group meditation fosters a stillness felt both in the atmosphere and within. It feels worshipful and calm. But in this room at the Lee Ufan Museum, there is no fine art to worship. This tranquillity is embedded into the space. There are no traditional prompts for sitting – no beanbags, benches, chairs, or even rugs, carpeting or turf – just the hard surface of the floor. So then what is the nature of this phenomenon – a collective, quiet resting – in this particular space?

One way of understanding this moment is that the boundaries between external/internal and me/other that I have created in order to conceive of 'myself' as an assemblage whole, have been absorbed into the atmosphere. Of course, atmospheres are fragile and dynamic, and my immersion ends in this realisation. Nonetheless, the processes of the affective assemblage, closely tied to atmosphere and sensory immersion, afford the visitor component the capacity to navigate the borderlines between that which is otherwise constructed as internal or external to the body. Consider Bachelard's proposition, that our capacity for a response is first feeling and then thought, a reaction that comes from the soul before it is caught in the mind. As a researcher, this visceral experience is a difficult one to catch. It exists in counteraction to traditional frames of knowledge, for capturing a 'reverberation' of feeling before it enters into a realm of personal or historical narrative. And yet, as evidenced in my own reflections from the Lee Ufan Museum, 'After the original reverberation, we are able to experience resonances, sentimental repercussions, reminders of our past. But the image has touched the depths before it stirs the surface' (Bachelard 1958: 8).

Breaking down the habitual distinctions between exteriority and interiority through embodied experience is not always realised in the visitor component of the affective assemblage. However, it can be argued that the processes and practice territorialising this assemblage pre-dispose this capacity. The resources in normative and responsive museums – signage, security, wall plaques – all exercise a rationalising role. The resources in affective museums, which engage haptic processes, exercise a sensory role. While somewhat paradoxical, due to the heavy spatial mediation by curators, the potentiality this holds for the visitor component is an extended temporal immersion into atmosphere.

Here, visitors play a clear territorialising role. Responding to environmental cues and the ambient atmospherics created by the artwork and the architecture, visitors move softly and quietly through the space. Alternatively, we could reverse this causal relation, saying that the soft and quiet movement of visitors through the space creates an atmosphere of tranquillity that impacts our perception of the artwork and architecture. Of course, it is a combination of all these relations working harmoniously. If one room contained a flashing neon artwork and a harsh noise soundscape it would have been as dissonant as a brash visitor running and shouting through the space. We can connect this assertion to the exploration of individual–collective experience explored earlier in 'publics', through my repeat visitation of Sammlung Boros.

In the Lee Ufan Museum, we see that tactile interaction is minimal (artworks were not accessible to touch), and there was certainly no 'sensory overload' in the way we have come to understand in 'spectacle'. There were no 'interactive' exhibits in the way we have commonly come to know them – no screens and no need to 'activate' an artwork through participation. Yet again, we can confirm that these components hold relations of exteriority. They can be present or absent from an assemblage system because it is the relation between components and not the components themselves that produce the assemblage. Ufan's conceptual approach places objects in 'communion' with each other. It wasn't until after leaving the museum that I reflected on the final room and had the realisation (or rationalisation) that we had positioned ourselves in the place of the objects to commune with the space. Had this concept been literally signposted, and had the visitor been asked to sit by museum staff, I doubt they would have been able to immerse themselves in the atmospheric presence. Nor would it have felt as though a learning experience had been accessed in an embodied and experiential way.

The simple act of taking of one's shoes to enter the final room of Lee Ufan has vast affective resonances, and showcases a complex set of relations. The taking off of one's shoes can prompt a subconscious or conscious connection to the atmospheres of other places. Margit Brünner (2015: 150) writes on how atmospheres contain other atmospheres, creating resonances between disparate locations. In this instance, I am thinking namely of the 'home', which in many cases (though, admittedly, not all) holds connotations of security and refuge. It could also be resonant with religious ritual, such as entering into a temple to pray. The small bench to place one's shoes under – across from the entrance of the final room in the Lee Ufan Museum – is so familiar, that one barely registers it, following the prompt in a borderline subconscious way. Yet as a component of the museum, it exercised a material role that played an integral role in territorialising the assemblage as affective. In the Lee Ufan Museum, there was no exposure to textual information in the final room of the exhibition space, but nonetheless we can discern a common response from visitors. Through this, we can reaffirm that the visitor component territorialises the affective assemblage through their immersion in the atmospherics of a museum's space.

Re-territorialising the Affective Museum

While we see instances of normative and responsive museums re-territorialising as affective assemblages, the same also occurs in reverse. One example of a museum that established itself as affective before re-territorialising as normative is the MAXXI in Rome. Following from the fashionable trend of arts-led urban regeneration in the 1990s, MAXXI was conceived as a national government project. With the completion of its award-winning building, designed by 'starchitect' Zaha Hadid, MAXXI opened to the public in 2010, with curator Hou Hanru appointed as the museum's artistic director.

At this point in time, the permanent collection of MAXXI had not yet been installed and Hanru had an opportunity (and challenge) that few museum curators are given: an empty museum. Hanru decided to 'reintroduce emptiness' as a statement against obsession and fetishism with materiality and consumption, using sound to transform the building (Hanru 2016). Each gallery was allocated to an artist to produce a thematic work, which became indicative of urban zones, to conceptually reflect how a contemporary city works and overlaps. The exhibition, titled *Open Museum/Open City* also had an open call, inviting people to contribute their own sound and facilitating a radio station takeover for the duration of six weeks. Events in the space included performances, narrative storytelling and public forums, creating 'encounters' and relational experiences. In fact, Hanru prefers to think of *Open Museum/Open City* as 'event', rather than 'exhibition' (Hanru 2016). Hanru noted the durational experience and immersive capacity of sound – in other words, its affective potential.

After *Open Museum/Open City*, MAXXI's permanent collection of twentieth- and twenty-first-century art was installed, described as a 'nucleus that witnesses the national and international artistic production, with special attention to the experiences and realities that are linked to the Italian context' (MAXXI: Art Collections n.d.). The architecture itself remains quite affective, in that the linear steel beams of the roof and the curved walls prompt the navigational flow (much like an airport). However, wall signage accompanies the works, the collection is arranged thematically, and seating is available for restive moments or contemplation of the art. Further, its mission statement expresses normative priorities, most notably, nation-building, 'promoting the current creative expressions of a nation such as Italy, characterised by centuries of primacy in the artistic and architectural fields' and 'intends to be a form of antenna transmitting Italian contents to the outside world while at the same time receiving from the outside the flux of international culture' (MAXXI: Mission Statement n.d.). Thus, the desiring code, the implementation of visual regimes in display, policies surrounding collection care and management, a hierarchical management system, their status as a 'publicly controlled private corporation' (in accordance with Italy's anti-corruption legislation) and consequential institutional regulations, all serve to re-territorialise MAXXI as normative.

We also have instances of affective assemblages re-territorialising as responsive assemblages. We can look towards the Centro de Arte Contemporânea Inhotim (hereafter Inhotim). Inhotim is located in the Brumadinho municipality of Brazil and is the creation of mining magnate Bernardo de Mello Paz. Inhotim began to be conceived in the mid-1980s, starting its trajectory as a private botanical garden designed by the Brazilian landscape architect Roberto Burle Marx. Gradually it evolved into a 5,000-acre garden, housing two-dozen art pavilions and over 500 artworks, a couple of shops, several restaurants and bars, with a hotel soon to be added to the list of on-site facilities. Inhotim is exceedingly participatory, with installations to walk through and rest in, like *Continente/Nuvem* (2008) by Rivane Neuenschwander, featuring cloud-like shapes floating on the ceiling to encourage a lie-down. There are also installations to swim in, like *Piscina* (2009) by Jorge Macchi and the cold pool in *Galeria Cosmococa*, popularly known as 'the kids gallery'. The participatory elements extend beyond a reactive engagement with the works and into an active collaboration in forming the installations. This is well expressed through *A Origem da Obra de Arte* (2002), a work conceptualised and started by artist Marilá Dardot, which sees visitors choose ceramic letter forms and seeds in order to 'grow words' in a field.

The connection to the environment surrounding it, as well as its participatory art collection and display, formed Inhotim as an affective assemblage. However, while Inhotim began as an affective museum in the late 1980s, it can be seen to shift into a responsive museum with the foundation of the Instituto Cultural Inhotim in 2002. Inhotim's status went from a private museum to a public institute, with an annual budget and a board of directors in 2008, though continues to be financed by Paz. Consequently, the museum structure changed from that of a private museum to a Public Interest Civil Society Organisation (OSCIP). As indicated in the previous chapter, when we look to the responsive museum assemblage, we see the educative role of the museum coming to the fore. It may still be participatory, but Inhotim's priorities became firmly solidified as community-engaged, revolving around opportunities for urban regeneration, which ultimately saw a shift in its 'desiring code' (values and mission) that aligns its practices (presenting a 'common notion') with the responsive assemblage.

Notes

1   See Böhme 1993; Radywyl 2008; Baker 2010; Papastergiadis 2013.
2   While owner–collector of Sammlung Boros, Christian Boros.

References

Bachelard, Gaston (1958). *The Poetics of Space*. M. Jolas (trans.) (1964) Reprint with foreword by M.Z. Danielewski and introduction by R. Kearney (2014). New York: Penguin Books.

Baker, Janice (2010). *Affect and Desire: Museums and the Cinematic*. Doctoral dissertation, Curtin University of Australia.

Benesse Art Site (n.d.). https://benesse-artsite.jp/en/about/, last accessed 10 November 2015.

Benesse Art Site: Lee Ufan Museum (n.d.). https://benesse-artsite.jp/en/art/leeufan. html, last accessed 08 December 2015.

Berger, John (1972). *Ways of Seeing*. 2008 Re-Issue. London/New York: Penguin.

Biehl-Missal, Brigitte and Dirk vom Lehn (2015). 'Aesthetics and Atmosphere in Museums: A Critical Marketing Perspective'. Michelle Henning (ed.) *International Handbook of Museum Studies: Museum Media*. Malden/Oxford: Wiley Blackwell. Pp. 235–258.

Böhme, Gernot (1993). 'Atmosphere as the Fundamental Concept of a New Aesthetics'. *Thesis Eleven* 36. Pp. 113–126.

Bourriaud, Nicolas (1998). *Relational Aesthetics*. S. Pleasance, F. Woods and M. Copeland (trans.) (2002). France: Les presses du reel.

Brünner, Margit (2015). *Constructing Atmospheres: Test-Sites for an Aesthetic of Joy*. Baunach, Germany: Impressum/Colophon.

Candlin, Fiona (2010). *Art, Museums and Touch*. Manchester/New York: Manchester University Press.

Cox, Rupert (2015). 'There's Something in the Air: Sound in the Museum'. Michelle Henning (ed.) *International Handbook of Museum Studies: Museum Media*. Malden/Oxford: Wiley Blackwell. Pp. 215–234.

Dardot, Marilá. (2002). *A Origem da Obra de Arte*. Inhotim, Brazil. Installation. Earthenware, plant pots in the shape of letters, soil, seeds, gardening tools.

Dudley, Sandra (2010). *Museum Materialities: Objects, Engagements, Interpretations*. Oxon & New York: Routledge.

Duncan, Carol (1995). *Civilising Rituals: Inside Public Art Museums*. London & New York: Routledge.

Grewcock, Duncan (2014). *Doing Museology Differently*. London/New York: Routledge.

Hächler, Beat (2015). 'Museums as Spaces of the Present: The Case for Social Scenography'. N. Hoskin (trans.). Michelle Henning (ed.) *The International Handbooks of Museum Studies: Museum Media* . Malden/Oxford: Wiley Blackwell. Pp. 349–370.

Hanru, Hou (2016). *AutoTune Everything Symposium*. Greek Centre, Melbourne, 19 August.

Hohmann, Silke (2013). 'A Talk with Christian and Karen Boros'. Boros Foundation (ed.) *Boros Collection Bunker Berlin, Volume 2*. Berlin: Distanz. Pp. 24–34.

Jackson, Antony and Jenny Kidd (2012). *Performing Heritage*. Manchester: Manchester University Press.

Kidd, Jenny (2014). *Museums in the New Mediascape: Transmedia, Participation, Ethics*. Surrey/Burlington: Ashgate Publishing, Ltd.

Lapp, Axel (2019). 'Interview with Christian Boros'. https://www.sammlungboros. de/press/clippings/art-review-1208, last accessed 23rd January 2020.

Macchi, Jorge. (2009). *Piscina*. Inhotim, Brazil. Installation. White cement and granite.

MAXXI: Art Collections (n.d.). https://www.maxxi.art/en/arte/, last accessed 3 August 2016.

MAXXI: Mission Statement (n.d.). https://www.maxxi.art/en/mission/, last accessed 3 August 2016.

Nakashima Degarrod, Lydia (2010). 'When Ethnographies Enter Art Galleries'. Sandra Dudley (ed.) *Museum Materialities: Objects, Engagements, Interpretations*. Oxon/ New York: Routledge. Pp. 128–142.

Nazareth, Paulo. (2013). *Arma Branca*. Sammlung Boros, Berlin. Woodcut on journal paper and wood. Viewed July 19, 2018.

Neuenschwander, Rivane. (2008). *Continente/Nuvem*. Inhotim, Brazil. Installation. Polypropylene sheets, aluminium, styrofoam balls, fluorescent lamps, electric fans.

Papastergiadis, Nikos (2013). *Ambient Perspectives*. Australia: Everbest.

Radywyl, Natalia (2008). *Moving Images, the Museum and a Politics of Movement: A Study of the Museum Visitor*. Doctoral Dissertation, The University of Melbourne, School of Culture and Communications & School of Historical Studies.

Radywyl, Natalia, Amelia Barikin, Nikos Papastergiadis and Scott McQuire (2015). 'Ambient Aesthetics: Altered Subjectivities in the New Museum'. Kylie Message and Andrea Witcomb (eds.) *International Handbook of Museum Studies: Museum Theory*. London/New York: Routledge. Pp. 417–436.

Sailstorfer, Michael. (2012). *Himmel Berlin*. Sammlung Boros, Berlin. Installation. Tire truck inner tubes. Viewed July 16, 2016.

Tzortzi, Kali (2015). *Museum Space: Where Architecture Meets Museology*. London/ New York: Routledge.

Witcomb, Andrea (2013). 'Understanding the Role of Affect in Producing a Critical Pedagogy for History Museums'. *Museum Management and Curatorship* 28(3). Pp. 255–271.

6   The Emergent Museum

Dynamic, Hospitable, and Disruptive

'Emergence' is much discussed in contemporary literature around the museum. Often laced with a discourse of 'flexibility', of 'dynamism' and 'flux', this literature explores how museums exercise component interactions as relative to the normative assemblage. However, much of this literature lends itself more strongly to responsive and/or affective practices, highlighting the way in which museums have changed, rather than the ways in which the potential for change has been integrated as a cornerstone for past, present and future practice within an institution. In museums, change can appear premeditated, incidental, or both. However, when change is accommodated as an ongoing structural commitment, in other words, through emergence as a *constant* practice rather than a *current* practice, the emergent common notion presents itself.

The emergent museum is called as such because its practices both acknowledge and encourage the very concept of the museum as an assemblage. In other words, the idea of a constant process of 'becoming' is embedded in the capacity afforded to components to re-territorialise the assemblage whole. The 'emergent' is therefore not a reference to something new, but rather to the heightened potential of this museum assemblage as a process of emerging. The emergent museum acknowledges itself as an open system, dynamic and necessarily in a state of flux. By 'necessarily', I am referring to the reactive capacity of each of the components in the assemblage, which results in a museum assemblage that holds flexibility inherent to its structure, which in turn allows for potential rapidity (temporal scale) in the configuration and reconfiguration of the assemblage whole. The emergent assemblage is genuinely self-reflexive of its role as an assemblage. It conceives of itself as an open system and builds opportunities for disruption into its organisational structure.

Ultimately, what distinguishes the emergent from the normative (Chapter 3), responsive (Chapter 4), and affective (Chapter 5) are the spatial and temporal scales through which the emergent museum manifests. As opposed to other museum assemblages, which work to limit the capacity of components to exercise roles that would unsettle the assemblage whole, the emergent museum accounts for – and in some relations encourages – disruption. Key

DOI: 10.4324/9781003393719-7

to the emergent museum is the way in which the perceived threats to cultural authority arising from the push towards collaborative, democratic, and open practices have been approached. Rather than the traditional 'containment and control' strategy implemented by normative and responsive assemblages (which is evidenced through the lower levels of expressive capacity displayed by various material components), the emergent museum presents itself as both porous and dynamic (leading to the perception of a greater expressive capacity afforded to its components). The emergent can also be easily distinguished from the affective. While the affective museum takes a different focus to the normative and responsive assemblages by being predominantly sensorial, the emergent assemblage both references and is disruptive of the narratives that precede it.

Contemporary society is characterised by the dual features of individualisation and global society. We have seen an opening up of the institution to include more voices, while also further blurring boundaries of public and private. In comparison to the wider field of museums as institution, the emergent museum shifts at a more rapid rate, reacting to cultural prompts as they emerge. Our present moment is one defined by flux. According to Harmut Rosa, a collective sense of the present is becoming increasingly fragile as the periods of stability become less frequent, characterised by shorter, more isolated and episodic experiences, leading to a society 'rich' in experiences (immediate, momentary), but 'poor' in experience (accumulated knowledge) (Rosa 2005: 47). Beat Hächler takes this assertion and extends it to the space of the museum, which can be understood as 'a temporary zone of stability in which the present is represented, that is, constructed' (Hächler 2015: 355). However, in the emergent museum, instability is a key part of its practice. Here, the 'temporary zone of stability' is eschewed in favour of an exploration of the mechanisms through which we approach, cope with and respond to flux.

Claire Bishop (2013) presents two categories for the contemporary in relation to her work on 'radical museology'. The first is 'presentism: the condition of taking our current moment as the horizon and destination of our thinking' and the second, a 'dialectical method and politicized project with more radical understandings of temporality' (Bishop 2013: 6). Bishop's acknowledgement of the multiple and disjunctive temporalities is fundamental to understanding the dynamism of the emergent assemblage. The emergent museum's relationship to temporality can be viewed as another characteristic that highlights its dynamism. It is this ability to engage with, respond to, and enjoy its own flexibility that makes the emergent museum contemporaneous. This is apparent in the rotation of temporary exhibitions through emergent museums, as well as the addition of ephemeral art and event to the museum space.

In understanding the emergent museum, we can also look towards Gerald Raunig's (2009) third phase of institutional critique (for phases one and two, see Chapter 4). This phase is understood as a dynamic form of instituent practice (Raunig 2009). Whereas phase one and two are both now seen as part of the art institution, those working through instituent practice are inventing 'new forms of instituting' and creating new networks through this process (Raunig and Ray 2009: xvii). There is a duality that defines instituent practice – it seeks to be self-critical but does not distance itself from the institution. It uses strategies that re-organise and reinvent constituent power.

Over the last decade, several scholars have begun to consider how instituent practice may occur within the museum, by focusing on and embracing complexity and potentiality. Duncan Grewcock's (2014) 'relational museum', which sees museums as active-dynamic rather than reactive-fixed, moves in this direction. Hächler (2015) approaches the understanding of museum space, not as a container, but as an arrangement of relationships and as a means of engineering certain performative possibilities. The dynamism and potentiality for museums and their visitors is likewise explored within the 'interrogative museum' articulated by Ivan Karp and Corinne Kratz (2015), which offers museum-goers' problems, rather than solutions, to showcase the multivalent nature of knowledge as well as provide space for dialogue. The interrogative museum challenges the claims to authority that the museum makes, both in terms of cultural authority and exhibitionary authority. Through the interrogative museum we begin to see the shadow of visitor feedback loops, whereby the visitor is given a platform and afforded enough agency to impact upon curatorial strategies within the museum.

Instituent practice can also be attached to Message's (2018) work, on the 'disobedient museum', which draws on interdisciplinary frameworks, critiques and strategies to assess the potentiality of the museum for political impact. Within this we can recognise Raunig's stipulation that contemporary institutional critique must 'link up with other forms of critique both within and outside the art field'. This is a necessary assertion, as contemporary critique needs to be as dynamic as the world it seeks to comprehend and challenge. It invokes working in the 'in-between' as an effective critical strategy. For the components that make up the emergent assemblage, this opens up the capacity of the components to exercise their roles, producing inconsistencies, outliers and new lines of flight. Throughout this chapter, I explore the Stapferhaus Lenzburg in Switzerland, and the Van Abbemuseum in Eindhoven to elucidate the way in which we can discern emergent practices.

Emergent Museum Priorities

Experimental, open, hospitable, defiant, dynamic – these make up the driving ideologies of the emergent assemblage. Take, for example, the Van Abbemuseum. The museum website self-proclaims that the Van Abbemuseum 'has an experimental approach towards art's role in society. Openness, hospitality and knowledge exchange are important to us' (Van Abbemuseum n.d.). This expresses several of the key foundations for an emergent assemblage. 'Openness' has strong resonance with the concept of assemblage itself. Its implications are that the museums' metaphorical borders and boundaries are porous and mutable. 'Hospitality' is a concept understood by Van Abbemuseum director Charles Esche in way that is contrary to the commonly presumed bidirectional roles between host and guest. Esche positions hospitality as being accommodating to 'the point of giving up authorship' (Žerovc 2015 [2003]: 158–159). He also expresses that 'Wholistic, inclusive and deviant [these] are the values we [Van Abbemuseum] have' (Esche: Interview, 2016).

Transgression and deviance are also aligned with defiance. Sebastian Olma (2018) writes that we can understand defiance as 'the will to open up the course of the world to the possibility of future deviation' (Olma 2018: 44). This aligns with the way we think about interactions within the emergent assemblage. If we consider what I noted earlier regarding the emergent assemblage's relationship to the 'present', what we see through emergent priorities and processes is a resistance to the persistent orientations towards progress and future that preoccupy the modernist perspective. Stapferhaus Lenzberg situates itself firmly in relation to the present. Stapferhaus was founded in the 1960s as a series of conferences and debates held in the Schloss Lenzburg (Lenzburg Castle), where people from diverse backgrounds could meet and discuss issues.[1] This history continues to shape its priorities today:

> With its exhibitions, the Stapferhaus Lenzburg creates room for dealing with contemporary questions. Workshops, events and publications allow for thematic deliberations for different target groups. At the same time, the Stapferhaus appeals to the audience and invites you to take your own position. As a kind of laboratory for the art of life, the Stapferhaus makes the difficult accessible and leads to connections without delivering prefabricated answers. In this way, Stapferhaus exhibitions make the present recognisable and negotiable.
>
> (Stapferhaus Lenzburg n.d.)

What distinguishes the emergent assemblage's relationship to the present from the affective assemblage is that in the former the sense of the present as outside of (individual) feeling is heightened. While affect certainly has a social dimension, the insularities of the affective assemblage are more prominent, while in the emergent assemblage, the social dimensions of museum visitation take on a wider scope (as seen through the feedback loops explored in relation to Mona in Chapter 1, and expanded upon later in this chapter).

Emergent Museum Resources

While we saw in the normative assemblage a tendency to conform to a 'white cube' grouping of resource components, the museums explored through this chapter deviate from this. Hächler positions the white cube in opposition to the museum-as-laboratory, writing that the latter is how we need to think about museums 'as a space of the present' (2015: 353). Tony Bennett (2013) explores the analogy of museum as laboratory in order to highlight the 'productive power of institutions'. The 'laboratory' rhetoric ties into another key concept that infuses the common notion of the emergent assemblage: experimentation. Arrangements between object and persons are repositioned in 'staged encounters'. While Bennett problematises this analogy 'because visitors practice their own forms of often quite unpredictable agency' (2013: 55), we can also conceivably argue that this is precisely the 'experiment' of the emergent museum. The interplay between complex systems of behaviour and changing conditions, characterised by inter-dependencies, complicates the dynamics of relations within the museum. 'Experimentation', through an assemblage lens, affords resource components the capacity to exercise a set of roles that produces different interactions and affects back on the assemblage.

Stapferhaus Lenzburg in Switzerland is a museum that has no permanent collection. In addition, for many years it had no permanent exhibition space, and it utilised a work crew from outside traditional museum professions. Instead of a collection and permanent location, it presented thematic exhibitions in specially chosen venues. In 1992, the new head of the Stapferhaus, Hans Ulrich Glarner, oversaw an implementation of new strategy, whereby the focus of Stapferhaus as a site for 'human encounters and intellectual debate' (Stapferhaus Lenzberg n.d., *own translation*) was positioned less as 'a cathedral' and more as a 'market' (Stapferhaus Lenzberg n.d., *own translation*). While Stapferhaus has now found a permanent home, these earlier practices are reminiscent of the ideologies of both Alexander Dorner and André Malraux in the late 1940s. Dorner's 1947 proposal for galleries at the Graduate School of Design at Harvard exemplifies how space was re-conceptualised for a fluid, rather than static, exhibition of art. He envisioned a space with no fixed walls in order to present art history with such flexibility that it becomes 'an action, a process', rather than a fixed form (Dorner 1947: 232 in Nesbit 2013: 45). The same year, André Malraux's *Musee imaginaire* explored the capacity for art to exist outside of time and place, a capacity closely linked to the affordances of photography (Meijers 1996: 10). For Malraux, the museum without walls was an exciting possibility afforded by technologies of reproduction. This allowed for an archive of art that could be reshuffled outside the constraints of time and place, finding new arrangements and connections within visual culture. Malraux saw his 'museum without walls' as offering the potential to disrupt the internal coherence established by museums and art historians to organise art and artefacts.

The temporary nature of the Stapferhaus, the lack of permanent collection and building, the focus on questions rather than answers, processes of collaboration and the visitor response all locate it as an emergent museum. While debates in museology have at times centred around the idea of the museum as a 'mausoleum', as a dead space filled with dead objects, which are seen lose their liveness by entering the institutionalised body, the emergent museum presents as a living space. The component relations of interiority and exteriority are particularly fluid in the emergent assemblage. While some resource components are absent, in other moments resources are added. Esche gives insight into this:

> In the current exhibitions we've developed a whole series of tools that–we call it a tool shop – and you can pick up various tools, which can take you around the exhibition. Some are developed by artists, so one is about standing on your head in the museum, or you take a yellow cushion and you go around and there are certain points where you take different viewpoints, so it's very much about physicality which we are going further into. So not only intellectual engagement but you lie down, or you stand up, push yourself right up into the corner of the space.
>
> (Esche: Interview, 2016)

The incorporation of different resource components into the spatiality of the museum increase the capacity of other components to act. As such, the visitor component, the artwork component and the architectural component are all afforded different kinds of material and expressive roles that align with the common notion of the emergent assemblage as a space for experimentation.

The shift towards more socially oriented approaches began in the Van Abbemuseum in the mid-1970s, with the appointment of Rudi Fuchs as director. Fuchs saw the role of the museum as an instrument for social change, unlike his predecessor Jean Leering, who proclaimed the autonomy (and elevated status) of art (Van Abbemuseum n.d.). However, during Fuchs time as director, the focus remained on collecting works that underscored significant artistic developments of the twentieth century. Following Fuchs, Jan Debbaut (director from 1988 to 2003) was mainly concerned with 'the relevance of visual art on the interface of modernism and postmodernism' until 1995, where 'the focus shifted to a somewhat younger generation, the emphasis being placed on audiovisual or somewhat more process-oriented work' (Van Abbemuseum n.d.). It was not until 2004, when Charles Esche took over from Debbaut as the Van Abbemuseum's Director that the museum's practices began to indicate emergent relational qualities. The capacity for a museum director to affect other component interactions is highlighted here. Beti Žerovc writes of Esche's career trajectory through the 1990s that his 'distinctive politically committed curatorial position' forged a personal brand, which institutions would recognise as shaping the direction of their institution if they were to appoint him (Žerovc 2015: 149). Accounts of Esche's work at various art institutions (Rooseum in Malmö, Witte de With in Rotterdam) lend support to this idea of the director component as a potentially destabilising/re-territorialising resource in the museum. Esche himself has said, 'When I first introduced some of these ideas the people working in the museum were kind of horrified so there was a lot of internal persuasion to do' (Esche: Interview, 2016).

The final resource I will highlight here is that of digital media. By positioning digital media as an extension of marketing and education, normative museums make efforts to retain the territorialisation of the assemblage. The emergent museum assemblage, on the other hand, is more porous. This porosity can be seen through new media forms in a greater platform use and response options (e.g. public comments enabled). When Lynda Kelly writes about the 'transformative museum' (2013: 55), she does so in the context of museums in the digital era, fundamentally linking the notion of transformation to the affordances of new forms of sociality, mobility and digital media (social networking services and other online platforms, like museum websites). While an engagement with digital media does not automatically qualify interactions between museum visitors and the sites of the museum as being indicative of the emergent assemblage, what is important about Kelly's argument is that it underscores the potentiality of these forms of interaction for dynamism, which is the cornerstone of emergent practice.

Emergent Museum Publics

Multiplicities

What is most notable about the emergent museum assemblage is that visitors to the museum are encouraged to explore multiple modalities along the spectrums of both participative immersion to spectatorship, and constituency to consumerism. Sometimes, this even extends to a literal 'role-playing', as was the case with the Van Abbemuseum's *Play* exhibition (2009–2011), where visitors were asked to choose between an experience of the exhibition as a flaneur, tourist, or pilgrim. Furthermore:

> There were certain points where you could change roles, you could change from being a pilgrim to a flaneur, so many people tried to do more than one. Once they got into the game it was kind of fun, there was a pleasure in doing.
>
> (Esche: Interview, 2016)

Visitor participation in museums is a loose term. In many cases, most notably within normative practice, participation is conflated with 'taking part'. In the responsive museum assemblage, participation included invitations to the museums' community to observe and, in some cases, shape decision-making. In affective assemblages, participation relates primarily to sensory immersion. In the emergent museum, visitor participation goes beyond this, invoking practices that share authority and power, and reshape the boundaries between professional and public through a greater affordance for the latter components capacity to affect in interactions. For example:

> I've been at the Van Abbe for twelve years, and it's definitely an unfolding narrative. So for instance that idea of the user was not there at the beginning, and many of the concepts have evolved partly as a result of experience, so you have a sort of feedback loop where you see what works and what doesn't. And I think that's been very important. So we've got to a position where we are, not through sort of rigorous repetition which would be in a way the modernist discourse, but actually by finding out where things are working and where they're not.
>
> (Esche: Interview, 2016)

Allowing for trial and error, as the above quote implies, is distinctly at odds with the 'control and containment' attitude seen within the normative assemblage. Making space for disruption, challenging authoritative narratives, and shifting away from 'rigorous repetition' all indicate a willingness to explore multiplicities.

Communication, Networks, and Feedback

Museum resources are communicated to the public via a range of special publications, instead of (sometimes in addition to) exhibition catalogues. We see this with Stapferhaus Lenzburg's *Begleitmagazin*. We also see resources communicated through their use of digital media (Kelly 2013: 60). A networked public is core to our understanding of the emergent assemblage. The potentiality for this is evident when we connect to Stephen Bann's argument that one way in which we could reflect the original flexibility of use (and meaning) in a curiosity cabinet would be to implement a hypertext strategy, uploading the entire collection online and allow for connections that are indicative of the collections 'relationship to diverse areas of knowledge' (Bann 2008: 124). However, unlike the curiosity cabinet, the flexibility of meaning in the emergent museum – through particular uses of social and mobile media – takes on the potential of personalisation on a wider scale (rather than the individual owner–collector), new geo-spatial forms, and different modes of sociality. It is also relevant to signpost that in addition to the usual event promotion, the Van Abbemuseum's Facebook page also shares political content. This creates a fluidity of place and time, a connection between local and global. It also situates the Van Abbemuseum reflexively within the wider context of our present moment. This is also observed through the linking of institutions. Once more, the Van Abbemuseum is an excellent example here, due in part to their relationship within the L'Internationale confederation. This has had implications for thinking about their publics in terms of a constituency. Aligned with what was discussed in relation to the responsive museum, art institutions have been questioning whether they 'have a constituency or just audiences' and invoking new practices of social engagement to overcome insularity (Graham 2018: 45). Esche states:

> And that idea of constituency and how you have dialogue with it, which isn't based on 'we have something to tell you' but what can we together figure out to use this public space for, is something that eventually I hope will develop what you're talking about, which is a feedback loop in which people feel they can express themselves, not only in terms of the collection and the work, but more importantly perhaps in what this public space of the museum means for them and how they've made use of it.
>
> (Esche: Interview, 2016)

The visitor feedback loop can be understood as the visitor component of an assemblage exercising both a material and expressive role and thus acting as its own system of interaction with the assemblage whole. Visitor feedback occurs on a variety of levels, through verbal and nonverbal communicative forms (movement, choice-making and engagement levels, spoken and written response). While the idea of 'feedback' is something that has been explored in museology since the turn towards visitor-centred studies in the 1990s, what is less explored is the continuation of this process, the feedback *loop*. By this, I mean not only the way in which visitors feed into the museum assemblage in an expressive capacity but also the way in which the museum assemblage absorbs this feedback and produces new iterations in response, which are responded to by museum visitors in a constant cycle. In light of assemblage theory, I see this feedback loop as the open system of one component, the visitor, intersecting with the open system of the assemblage, the museum.

The emergent museum assemblage seeks to 'foster' this feedback. In other words, it does not treat visitor participation as a natural and authentic source of (pre-existing) meaning, but as an important stimulus that has to be nurtured in order to be explored. The visitor feedback loop becomes a focal point in the emergent assemblage, as it encourages a perception of an enhanced capacity for components to affect back on the assemblage. It territorialises the emergent common notion as open, convivial, communicative, and dynamic.

Emergent Museum Processes

The way in which the various components explored above come together through processes can be aligned with the concept of the non-sequitur, as explored by Johanna Drucker. Drucker (2011) uses the principles of frame analysis to look at how we make 'meaningful relations among elements of interpretation' (Drucker 2011: 2). The non-sequitur is defined by its divergence from the linear narrative expressed in other 'framing' relations, relying instead on our cognitive ability to make connections between seemingly unrelated fragments. It also has implications for considering the practices of the emergent museum as 'rhizomatic' (Deleuze and Guattari 1987 [1980]). That is, they are multiple and non-hierarchical – 'between-things' that flow into new spaces, ceaselessly creating connections. These concepts take a particular relevance when considering component relations within the emergent assemblage, which are afford a greater fluidity in their capacity to both interpret and affect.

Drucker writes that non-sequitur connections are most evident in electronic space, where users shift between activities, embedded mediums (e.g. audio to video) and forms of communication (e.g. advertising to social networking) and further, are constantly offered alternatives to jump from one point of attention to another (2011: 4). I find this to be relevant in the way visitors are afforded the capacity to embody several different modes of visitation. As we move from a mode of spectatorship that rests in the rational/observational to the participatory/co-productive, the capacity of interfaces within the museum and their affective relationality with other components has changed.

Non-sequitur relations can be discerned through the processes occurring at the Van Abbemuseum. Over the last decade and a half, Van Abbemuseum has consistently challenged the linear modernist, Western narrative found in many museums. Esche reflects on this:

> [T]he metaphor that I always understood as *Plug In* was when I arrived at the museum it felt like the museum was a very perfect closed narrative . . . [*Plug In*] was about breaking down the coherent, chronological narrative, but also what I would understand now, and maybe I understood it also then but probably less coherently, as a modern narrative of endless growth and endless progress of Western and white dominance.
>
> (Esche: Interview, 2016)

This arises from a curatorial strategy that brings together resource components (in this case the collection) into a spatial configuration that aligns itself with a non-sequitur flow. Esche has stated:

> [W]e set about with the *Plug Ins'*, with this very deliberate attempt to smash the [modernist] narrative and to simply use each room as its own fragment– and those fragments just bucked against each other, struggled against each other– and see what survived. And it was really confusing for [the visitors]. So the first lesson we learnt was that by disregarding that narrative, or dismantling that narrative, or deconstructing that narrative, that modern narrative, the first reaction from people was to be lost. To the

extent that we would show the collection as *Plug In* and people would say 'Where's the collection?'

(Esche: Interview 2016)

Exhibits that disarm visitor expectation are useful tools in creating museum spaces that are socially performative. By disrupting the context and expectations associated with museum spaces, the emergent assemblage disrupts the visitor's perception of their own role. Beat Hächler (2015) posits that a 'museum as a space for the present' positions visitors in a scenario of contemplation. This is something we see across museum common notions. Unlike other common notions, however, this contemplation is about a confrontation with the self to create moments of reflection. The self-reflexivity of visitors in the emergent museum, affords the visitor component a greater capacity to affect the other components of the assemblage. In other words, the visitor is given a role that goes beyond the material and into the expressive. When we think of Michel de Certeau's concept of space as a 'practiced place' (1984: 117), the self-reflexivity of the emergent museum highlights the potentiality of 'becoming'. When the visitor is allowed the visitor-actor role in an exhibition, it imbues the space with a multiplicity. The museum becomes multiple spaces, 'depending on who is carrying out what actions' (Hächler 2015: 353). The component relations in Stapferhaus are indicative of what Hächler calls 'social scenography'. Social scenography gives agency to exhibitions, making their capacity to affect explicit. It is the structuring of content and the form of a spatial situation, but it relies on the development of a social situation in order to be invoked. In this way it is unable to be pre-formulated, it comes into existence through the interactions between participants – with the theme and each other. The material components of the museum become a prompt for the performative enactment of the theme and the realisation of an exhibition.

In 2006, Stapferhaus held a 12-month exhibition titled *Glaubensacche: Eine Ausstellung für Gläubige und Ungläubige (A Matter of Belief)* in a warehouse, which was later shown in the Luxembourg City History Museum. From the initial point of entering the exhibition, visitors were asked to position themselves as active, reflexive agents, by identifying themselves as 'believers' or 'nonbelievers' and walking through a corresponding entryway based on their decision. Ambiguous direction, the creation of an unsure mindset, asks the visitor to pause, reflect and question. What is being asked of me right now? What does it mean to believe? Believe in what? While other exhibits may speak more 'autonomously', asking the visitor to look, read and perhaps understand the artwork, other types of interactive exhibits (like the installed entry doors in *A Matter of Belief*) treat the objects as 'instructions for action' (Hächler 2015: 352). This kind of interpretive flexibility, as well as the ambiguity in direction (and therefore the self-responsibilitisation of movement), lends itself to relations shaped by curiosity. This invokes Steven

Bann, who has asserted the correlation between curiosity, and a 'secondary revision of value' through connections between objects and personal associations (2008: 125).

The link between curiosity and the revision of value is one that plays into component interactions between visitor and the material objects in museum spaces. The Deleuzian concept of a genuine 'encounter' can be invoked here. Simon O'Sullivan writes that a genuine encounter is when recognition shifts to re-cognition (2006: 1). Rather than having our knowledge and beliefs affirmed through recognition, re-cognition is disruptive, seen as posing a challenge to our systems of knowledge. Curiosity might be seen as a catalyst in this example, or an 'expressive' interaction (DeLanda 2006: 22) which triggers a capacity (system openness) for a genuine encounter. Like the affective assemblage, one of the key features of the emergent museum is that it provides an 'immersive experience' that surrounds the visitor. As such, it relates to multiple facets of the museum, from the architecture to the exhibitions. 'Immersion' also suggests a deep involvement in something and extends to practices of visitor participation and connection. There are layers to an immersive museum experience. First is the relationship between the museum architecture and its surrounding environment. Second is within the gallery, with a multiplicity of affordances shaping and being shaped by visitor movement around the space and their interaction (physical, emotional, intellectual) with artworks. It is immersion that plays the largest role in the emergent museums' focus on the sensory experience, doing so through architecture, lighting, installations and curation. The emergent museum visitor can be the art historian, the critical museum visitor, the academic, the tradesperson, the philistine, the child. The way the emergent museum visitor experiences and engages with the museum continues to depend on a mixture of habitus and openness, but there is no longer the same institutional weight placed on 'art worship', or a perceived need for a formal art education to 'properly' experience the museum.

An example of immersive experience and the sensory as curatorial strategy is the Van Abbemuseum's '*Plug In*' (2006–2008) exhibition. In one room, video works made by female artists in the 1960–1970s were displayed in a specially wallpapered and furnished gallery space. As a visitor, to best view the audio-visual works one had to sit on one of the available retro couches. In another room, artworks from the Van Abbe collection were displayed alongside an assortment of video games. It is the combination of reimagined gallery spaces with both sound and visuals and the unexpectedness of curatorial configurations provide the visitor with a sensory experience of the museum.

Openness, hospitality and knowledge exchange are important to us. . . . We challenge ourselves and our visitors to think about art and its place in the world, covering a range of subjects, including the role of the collection as a cultural 'memory' and the museum as a public site. International collaboration and exchange have made the Van Abbemuseum a place for creative cross-fertilisation and a source of surprise, inspiration and imagination for its visitors and participants.

(Van Abbemuseum n.d.)

When we continue with assemblage theory, the interplay of both structure and agency becomes not only traceable but also no longer fixed chronologically or institutionally. The return to curiosity, as well as the acknowledgement of the 'unstable' object and its network of meanings, are features of the Wunderkammer tradition that play to the dynamism of the emergent museum assemblage. These same characteristics of the curiosity cabinet – instability, precariousness, and openness of the object – give components of the emergent museum their perceived flexibility. This exploration of the Wunderkammer, with its particular focus on the object and the way in which the object was thought about and displayed, indicates yet another material component being situated with an expressive capacity. The object is recognised as flexible in the emergent museum, which acknowledges its ability to impact on, as well to be impacted by, the wider museum assemblage.

Media comes to play an important role in emergent museum practice. This is, in large part, due to the capacity to communicate information in a way not limited by the physicality of wall placards. As a result, it allows for a multiplicity of voices and views to be communicated. It also provides an access point for visitors to feedback into the museum. To this end, we come to the process of visitor feedback loops, which are a core component interaction found in the emergent museum assemblage. An emergent visitor feedback loop takes the process of visitor feedback (normally found in surveys, museum focus groups etc.) into the experience of the museum. It moves beyond informing marketing strategies and analysing 'audience' preferences, into shaping the museum assemblage as a whole. It takes on a particular importance in affecting engagement between visitors and museum staff, for example, in curatorial strategies, and engagement between visitors. At the Van Abbemuseum, this can be seen through the series of experimental negotiations between the museum visitor and the curator that made up the Van Abbemuseum exhibition from '*Plug In*' (2006) to '*Plug In to Play*' (2008). The final 18-month project is called '*Play Van Abbe*' (2009–2011) and it consisted of exhibitions, projects, performances, lectures, discussions, to prompt a critical reflection by the audience on the relations between art and society. It had a gamified element, positioning all human-components (visitor, artists, staff) in an active role that, through playful interactions in the space, could also lead to critical thought. In the small booklet produced as part of *Play Van Abbemuseum*, Esche is quoted saying;

'It is our ambition in the museum to create the conditions in which you as a visitor and participant are helped to think critically about the world as well as what we have done. At the same time, we hope you can enjoy the

experience of looking at works of art in our collection and feel empowered
to construct your own narratives around them.'

(Esche 2009: 5)

At the end of Play visitation, visitors were encouraged to come back to a computer screen in the exhibition space where, together with a volunteer (called
'game-masters') they could trace their journey through the museum. Further
to this, if the visitor engaged in a longer conversation, they were awarded a
badge, to showcase that you had been part of a process. This dramatically
opened the space for dialogue. Furthermore, volunteers are seen as an integral part of communicating visitor feedback to other points of interaction in
the museum, with Esche stating that the 'anecdotal stories' from volunteer
feedback sessions help in figuring out 'what works and what doesn't' (Esche:
Interview, 2016). The visitor feedback loop, a process whereby the visitor
communicates (directly or indirectly) to the museum, whereby communication is received and consequently impacts on curatorial strategies, exemplifies
the dynamism of the emergent museum.

The practice of reflexive thinking exists in the emergent museum as an
interesting addition to the role of the sensory. First, we have a point of contact that arouses the sense. Next we enter into curiosity and stimulation. We
also see it in Esche's juxtaposition of 'critical thinking' and 'enjoyment'. The
emergent art museum holds within it both a focus on the sensory and the experiential, as well as an emphasis on perspectivism. It is the response of both
feeling and thought that the emergent museum stimulates, that situates the
visitor as an individual and as part of a community. Thus far, through the normative, responsive and affective museum assemblages, we have seen a variety
of limitations and affordances in component relations, with varying capacities
to affect back on the assemblage. The emergent museum assemblage takes
more of a focus on the visitor components capacity to exercise relations, and
the potentiality within these.

As I noted earlier in this chapter, part of what territorialises the assemblage
as emergent, is a self-reflexivity of emergence. We have already shown the
way in which certain resource components (such as the museum director) are
considered to have a high-level capacity to affect. When this is paralleled by a
personal belief in the potentiality of things, we see said components working
towards dynamic practices. Esche has previously stated (Žerovc 2015 [2003]:
153) that the relationship he has with the concept of 'possibility' is crucial
to his work. It is through the internalisation of possibility that dynamism,
change, and new productive knowledges and actions take place.

The emergent museum is an immersive experience; it is collaborative,
simultaneously local and global in its reach, it makes continuous efforts
towards transparency, is self-reflexive and holds visitor feedback loops. In
relation to the emergent assemblage, other museum assemblages are a more

easily perceived as a common notion. The transience and precarity of the emergent assemblage as a common notion lend it a 'speculative' feel, leading us to question whether there is ever an emergent common notion, or whether this is an oscillation between the other three assemblages already outlined. The paradox of the emergent assemblage is that component relations are afforded more flexibility and, as a result, interactions can equally propel the assemblage towards a normative institutionalism or retain the dynamism of emergence. The key here, is how we observe a general cohesion among component relations towards a common notion across a consolidated spatial and temporal scale. All museums have the potentiality to re-territorialise as an assemblage common notion, often resulting in moments of hybridity between assemblages. However, 'moments' do not necessarily re-territorialise the common notion. Re-territorialisation effects the assemblage whole, only occurring through a sustained perception of the affordance or limitations in the component's capacity to affect. If the emergent assemblage is to remain territorialised as an emergent common notion, it must be perceived as persistently contradictory, and self-reflexive regarding its own dynamism.

Note

1   It wasn't until 1994 that the Stapferhaus began an exhibition format, and not until 2018 that they opened a permanent exhibition site in the former Lenzburg Station. Prior to this, their activities spread over multiple sites.

References

Bann, Steven (2008). 'The Return to Curiosity: Shifting Paradigms in Contemporary Museum Display'. A. McClellen (ed.) *Art and its Publics: Museum Studies at the Millennium*. Oxford: Blackwell Publishing Ltd. Pp. 117–130.

Bennett, Tony (2013). *Making Culture, Changing Society*. London: Routledge.

Bishop, Claire (2013). *Radical Museology*. London: Koenig Books.

De Certeau, Michel (1980 [1984]). *The Practice of Everyday Life*. S.F. Rendall (trans.). Berkeley/Los Angeles/London: University of California Press.

DeLanda, Manuel (2006). *A New Philosophy of Society: Assemblage Theory and Social Complexity*. London/New York: Continuum.

Deleuze, Gilles and Felix Guattari (1987 [1980]). *A Thousand Plateaus*. B. Massumi (trans.). London: Continuum.

Dorner, Alexander. (1947). *The Way Beyond 'Art' - the Work of Herbert Bayer*. New York: Wittenborn.

Drucker, Johanna (2011). 'Humanities Approaches to Interface Theory'. *Culture Machine* 12. Pp. 1–20.

Esche, Charles. (2009). 'Introduction'. *Plug in to Play*. Eindhoven: Van Abbemuseum. Exhibition Catalogue. P. 5.

Esche, Charles (2016). 'Interview with Jasmin Pfefferkorn'. *Melbourne*, last accessed 9 November 2016.

Graham, Janna (2018). 'Negotiating Institutions'. John Byrne, Elinor Morgan, November Paynter, Aida Sánchez de Serdio and Adela Z!eleznik (eds.) *The Constituent Museum*. Amsterdam: Valiz. Pp. 44–49.

Grewcock, Duncan (2014). *Doing Museology Differently*. London/New York: Routledge.

Hächler, Beat (2015). 'Museums as Spaces of the Present: The Case for Social Scenography'. N. Hoskin (trans.). Michelle Henning (ed.) *The International Handbooks of Museum Studies: Museum Media*. Malden/Oxford: Wiley Blackwell. Pp. 349–370.

Karp, Ivan and Corinne A. Kratz. (2015). 'The interrogative museum'. Raymond A. Silverman (ed.) *Museum as Process: Translating Local and Global Knowledges*. London/ New York: Routledge. Pp. 279–298.

Kelly, Lynda (2013). 'The Connected Museum in the World of Social Media'. K. Drotner and K. Schroder (eds.) *Museum Communication and Social Media: The Connected Museum*. London: Routledge. Pp. 54–71.

Meijers, Debora J. (1996). 'The Museum and the 'Ahistorical' Exhibition: the latest gimmick by the arbiters of taste, or an important cultural phenomenon?'. Reesa Greenburg, Bruce W. Ferguson and Sandy Nairne (eds.). *Thinking About Exhibitions*. London/ New York: Routledge. Pp. 5–14.

Message, Kylie. (2018). *The Disobedient Museum: Writing at the Edge*. London/ New York: Routledge.

Nesbit, Molly. (2013). *The Pragmatism in the History of Art*. Pittsburgh: Periscope Publishing.

Olma, Sebastian (2018). *Art and Autonomy: Past Present Future*. Rotterdam: V2_Publishing.

O'Sullivan, Simon (2006). *Art Encounters Deleuze and Guattari: Thought Beyond Representation*. Hampshire/New York: Palgrave Macmillan.

Raunig, Gerald (2009). 'Instituent Practices: Fleeing, Instituting, Transforming'. G. Raunig and G. Ray (eds.) *Art and Contemporary Critical Practice: Reinventing Institutional Critique*. London: MayFlyBooks. Pp. 3–12.

Raunig, Gerald and Gene Ray (eds.). (2009). *Art and Contemporary Museum Practice: Reinventing Institutional Critique*. London: MayFlyBooks.

Rosa, Harmut (2005). *'Beschleunigung: Die Veränderung der Zeitstrukturen in der Moderne' [Acceleration: The Alteration of Time Structures in the Modern World]*. Frankfurt: Suhrkamp.

Stapferhaud Lenzburg (n.d.). 'Stapferhaus Lenzburg: About'. https://www.stapferhaus.ch/stapferhaus/, last accessed 17 October 2017.

Van Abbemuseum (2009). *Plug in to Play*. Exhibition catalogue. Eindhoven: Van Abbemuseum.

Van Abbemuseum (n.d.). https://vanabbemuseum.nl, last accessed 11 August 2018.

Žerovc, B. (2015). *When Attitudes Become the Norm: The Contemporary Curator and Institutional Art*. Ljubljana and Berlin: Archive Books.

Index

Note: Page numbers in *italics* indicate a figure on the corresponding page.

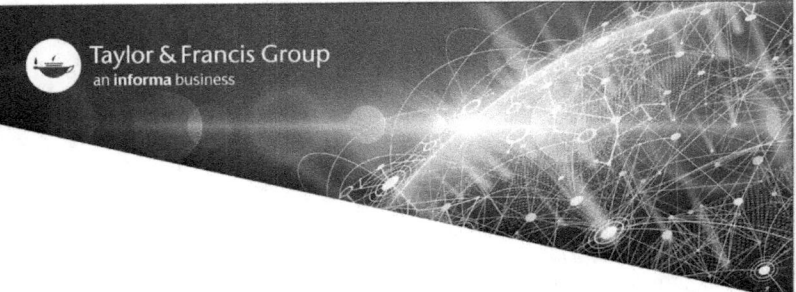
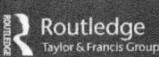
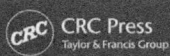

For Product Safety Concerns and Information please contact our EU
representative GPSR@taylorandfrancis.com
Taylor & Francis Verlag GmbH, Kaufingerstraße 24, 80331 München, Germany

www.ingramcontent.com/pod-product-compliance
Lightning Source LLC
Chambersburg PA
CBHW072210170526
45158CB00002BA/535